EASY THAI
COOKBOOK

Sallie Morris

EASY THAI
COOKBOOK

Sallie Morris

OVER **70** DELICIOUSLY SIMPLE RECIPES

NOURISH

EAT WELL, LIVE WELL

First published in the United Kingdom and Ireland in 2007 by Duncan Baird Publishers Ltd.

This edition published in the UK and USA in 2018 by Nourish, an imprint of Watkins Media Limited
19 Cecil Court
London WC2N 4EZ
enquiries@nourishbooks.com

Copyright © Watkins Media Limited 2007, 2010, 2018
Text © Sallie Morris 2007, 2010, 2018
Photography © Watkins Media Limited 2007, 2010, 2018

The right of Sallie Morris to be identified as the Author of this text has been asserted in accordance with the Copyright, Designs and Patents Act of 1988.

Managing Editor: Grace Cheetham
Designers: Glen Wilkins and Karen Smith
Studio Photography: William Lingwood
Photography Assistant: Alice Deuchar
Stylists: Jenny White (food) and Helen Trent (props)

A CIP record for this book is available from the British Library

ISBN: 978-1-84483-893-6

10 9 8 7 6 5 4 3 2 1

Printed in China

Language notes

English and Thai names are used throughout the book. There is no definitive way to translate spellings from Thai to English because Thai is tonal. *Nam* can be *nahm*, *phed* can be *phet* and *tom khaa gai* can be *tom ga khai*. If in doubt, say the word out loud.

To my husband Johnnie for his love and support and enjoyment of Thai food.

Author's acknowledgements

Thanks to the following organizations, hotels, restaurants and individuals:
The Mandarin Oriental Hotel in Bangkok, and the Dhara Dhevi in Chiang Mai with cookery schools in both locations as well as The Blue Elephant where I gained friends and valuable information on the cuisine and fruit and vegetable carving. The Cape Panwa Hotel in Phuket, in whose company I visited markets and learned the art of napkin folding. In the UK, Khun Sitinan and his wife Sunanta were generous with their time and help, which was invaluable, and I thank them most sincerely. They run the Thai restaurant at The Golden Fleece, Elstead, Surrey. Another favourite restaurant is The Montien in Kew, Surrey, which has delighted us for 15 years with its consistent high standards in real Thai food cooked by Anna and served by Thomas and Karen. Phalida runs the Paya Thai Supermarket in Richmond, Surrey for the best Thai ingredients. Magimix food processors and steamers were and still are my top assistants in the kitchen. Finally, Grace Cheetham for encouraging me to write this book and Beryl Castles for secretarial help.

Publisher's note

While every care has been taken in compiling the recipes for this book, Watkins Media Limited, or any other persons who have been involved in working on this publication, cannot accept responsibility for any errors or omissions, inadvertent or not, that may be found in the recipes or text, nor for any problems that may arise as a result of preparing one of these recipes. If you are pregnant or breastfeeding or have any special dietary requirements or medical conditions, it is advisable to consult a medical professional before following any of the recipes contained in this book.

Notes on the recipes

Unless otherwise stated:
• Use medium eggs
• Use fresh herbs
• Do not mix metric and imperial measurements
• 1 tsp = 5ml; 1 tbsp = 15ml; 1 cup = 250ml

CONTENTS

INTRODUCTION

The popularity of Thai food is borne out by the ever-increasing number of Thai restaurants, as more people recognize the delicious mouth-tingling delights of real Thai cuisine. Originally the Thai (Tai) people were migrants from southwest China who first settled in the north and kept moving southward, setting up capitals with romantic names such as Sukhothai ("Dawn of Happiness"), Ayutthaya ("Unassailable") and then Bangkok ("City of Angels") at the end of the eighteenth century. On their move south, they found that the fertile central plains and plentiful rainfall proved perfect for paddy fields of superb quality, which is why the area is known as the rice bowl of Southeast Asia.

Thailand is about the size of France with a population of around 60 million. Myanmar, Laos, Cambodia and Malaysia are its immediate neighbours. With trade between these and other countries of the region, many ingredients are common to each cuisine but are frequently employed in entirely different cooking methods, neatly illustrating the point that food has no borders or boundaries. Though regional cooking exists in Thailand, Thai restaurants will more usually cook and serve the better known dishes that they know their customers will enjoy.

The development of Thai cuisine, with its historical and culinary influences from China, has been a long and subtle process. From Arab and Indian merchants, the Thais adopted the use of dry spices – coriander, cumin, nutmeg, cloves and turmeric – as used in the Thai Mussaman Curry (see page 98). This gave a new dimension to the work of the talented cooks of the royal household, which eventually developed into what is today one of the world's most exciting cuisines. Perhaps the most significant import was the chilli, which was brought east by the Portuguese. Its place in the cooking of Thailand is undisputed, but it is the clever way in which the different flavours are married together that makes Thai food unique. Threads of Indian cuisine are also revealed in the rich tapestry of Thai food. The wet spice pastes bear a strong resemblance to the masalas of southern India, which invariably include the essential three Cs of oriental cookery: coconut, chilli and coriander/cilantro.

The three overriding attractions of Thai food are the tastes, textures and aromas. The tastes include red and green hot bird's eye chillies; creamy coconut; coriander/cilantro (roots, stalks and leaves); basil leaves, with their aniseed aroma; heavenly lemon grass; pine-like galangal (kha); torn lime leaves (just smell that citrus fragrance); limes for their juice or as wedges to squeeze over prepared dishes; pungent kapi (fermented shrimp paste), which has no fishy taste but gives depth to dishes in which it is used; and salty, whisky-coloured fish sauce, *nam pla* – definitely *the* Thai condiment. The textures are crunchy peanuts and toasted desiccated/dried shredded coconut, crisp green vegetables and unripe fruits for salads such as green mango, meltingly tender deep-fried fish and curried meats, and juicy, simply prepared oriental fruits, such as mangosteens and lychees. As for the aromas, just the fragrance of lemon grass and lime leaves or the aroma of a curry paste being stirred into coconut milk is enough to whet the appetite.

An interest in food is always a joy – a never-ending voyage of discovery in which there is always something new around the corner. With the growing popularity of Thai cuisine, the ingredients are increasingly widely available, whether in supermarkets or corner shops, so, with the help of these recipes, you too can cook authentic Thai food.

THE BASICS

Thai cuisine involves ingredients that may be unfamiliar to some cooks, but virtually all of them will be available at large supermarkets, if you are not lucky enough to have an oriental store near you. Bamboo shoots, bean curd, bean sprouts, chillies, coconut, curry pastes, fish sauce and lemon grass all add their exotic flavours to Thai meals. "Rice" and "food" are synonymous in the Thai language, so a good helping of rice is central to the meal, unless noodles are being served.

The only specialist equipment you will need is a wok for stir-fries, though a pestle and mortar are useful for grinding pastes. Thai food is usually barbecued, deep-fried, steamed or stir-fried, all of which are quick methods of cooking, so the food will be ready in no time. Only curries, which need to simmer for a while to develop their flavours, take much time to cook. At the heart of Thai cookery lie the pastes on which so many delicious dishes are based: red and green curry pastes, Mussaman curry paste and Hung Lay curry paste all play an important part in the final flavour, though many have their spicy character subdued by the addition of coconut milk – a central ingredient in Thai food. Once you understand the basic ingredients and methods, you are ready to prepare your first Thai meal.

INGREDIENTS

AUBERGINES OR EGGPLANTS

These are also known as brinjal (a name of Indian origin). There are many different types, from the long purple variety to the white/green type, about the size of a ping-pong ball, which can be eaten raw with Nam Prik Sauce (see page 50), or pounded with the ingredients for a sauce or added to curries. The garden pea type can be used in the same way in the sauce or as an addition to a green curry.

BAMBOO SHOOTS

Sliced bamboo shoots are available in cans. Once the can is opened, pour the contents into a container with a lid, cover with fresh water daily and use within a week.

BANANA LEAVES

These giant leaves, used as the Southeast Asian answer to kitchen foil, are available from some oriental supermarkets. Plunge the leaves into boiling water to make them more supple before placing the ingredients that are to be cooked inside and folding the leaf over into a neat parcel. Often you will need a cocktail stick/toothpick or thin satay stick to secure the parcel. Food wrapped in this way is usually grilled/broiled or sometimes steamed, giving the food the added flavour of the banana leaf itself. Apart from the taste, foil is an acceptable alternative. Banana leaves can also be used as plates, as well as being made into cups to hold food during cooking (see page 26 for instructions).

BASIL LEAVES

There are three types of basil. Sweet basil (*bai horapha*) is used widely in curries and some stir-fry dishes. It has dark, glossy leaves with a strong, pungent flavour. Holy basil (*bai krapao*), so named because it flourishes around pagodas, has longer, narrower and lighter-coloured leaves. It gives off its full flavour, which is hot and spicy, quite like cloves, only when cooked and is much used as an ingredient in stir-fry dishes. Finally, lemon basil (*bai mangluk*) is popular in the northeastern region of Thailand in soups and salads.

BEAN CURD

Fragile-looking 7.5cm/3in squares of fresh bean curd, or tofu, are sold in the refrigerated section of oriental stores from an open box covered with fresh water. The bean curd is made from soybean milk set with gypsum. In spite of its bland flavour, it is full of protein and used throughout the whole region. It will keep in the refrigerator for three or four days if covered with fresh water daily. A long-life version is also available from supermarkets; once opened use as fresh. Deep-fried bean curd is used in many dishes. Cubes of bean curd, which are deep-fried until golden and packaged for the freezer, are available in 100g/3½oz bags from oriental stores. To use from the freezer, pour boiling water over them to thaw, drain after one minute, cool slightly and then squeeze the curd cubes to get rid of any excess oil. The cubes can then be used whole or cut into slices.

BEAN SPROUTS

Used throughout the East for their appearance and texture, bean sprouts are readily available from grocery stores and supermarkets. Choose only those sprouts that look fresh and white and have been kept in a cool place. To store, turn them out of the packaging and place in a container of cold water, changing this each day. Most bean sprouts come from mung beans, though soybean sprouts are also available. Removal of the brown root and sometimes the head makes them look more attractive but can be time-consuming and unnecessary, especially if they are to be added to a stir-fry or spring rolls.

Mung and soybeans can both be sprouted at home. Wash well and soak overnight, then drain and rinse again. Line a deep plastic tray with a few layers of damp paper towel, sprinkle with the mung beans and set in a warm, dark place such as the airing cupboard, covering with cling film/plastic wrap and maybe even a newspaper to keep out the light. Sprinkle with water every day for six to nine days until the sprouts are fully developed. Use as soon as possible or store in the refrigerator as above. Do not grow too many at once. From 50g/2oz mung beans you get 225g/8oz sprouts. For soybeans, follow the directions on the package.

CARDAMOM

Green or white pods are readily available. Clusters of the pods grow near ground level on a plant that is a member of the ginger family. To capture the full exquisite flavour, which is warm and pungent with a hint of lemon, dry-fry if the recipe suggests it, then bruise the pods and prise them open. Remove the tiny black seeds, which can be crushed and added to a range of dishes, particularly chicken.

CHILLIES

These are an indispensable ingredient. There are two main types in Thai cooking: the finger-sized chilli, *prik chii faa*, which comes in red or green and sometimes orange, and the tiny bird's eye, or scud, chilli, *prik khee noo*, which is even more powerful and is used extensively. Chilli addicts can even be seen eating these whole. Whichever type you are using, treat it with great respect as the oils from the chilli must not get near your lips or eyes as they will sting. To prepare for cooking, simply remove the cap from the chilli, then slit from top to bottom under running water and scoop out the seeds (unless you like your food fiercely hot). Use rubber gloves or wash your hands thoroughly with soap and water after preparation. Slice, then pound to a paste using a pestle and mortar or use a food processor.

You can buy a good-quality chilli paste sold by the name of *sambal ulek* (red chilli). Two fresh chillies are equivalent to one teaspoon of chilli paste.

Dried chillies are sold widely. They can be deseeded, then ground to a powder using a pestle and mortar or soaked in warm water for 15 minutes, then pounded into a paste.

Chilli powder is easily obtainable when all the other alternatives cannot be found. Buy little and often, and store away from the light so that it retains its flavour and colour.

CHINESE MUSHROOMS

Good-quality ones might seem expensive but they do add a distinctive flavour to a variety of dishes. They must be soaked in water for 20–30 minutes before being used. Remove, drain and discard the stems, then use the mushrooms whole or cut into slices. The soaking liquid can be used as stock or in soup.

CINNAMON

You can buy cinnamon either whole in sticks or ground, which is sold loose or in jars. Cinnamon is more widely associated with sweet dishes in the West but in the cooking of Southeast Asia its spicy fragrance is used in curries.

COCONUTS

Known as *ma prow*, or food of the gods, huge plantations are nurtured to produce the phenomenal quantities of coconut milk and cream required by Thailand's cooks. There is a big business in canning, freeze-drying and freezing the liquid for export. Coconut milk and cream can be homemade from desiccated/dried shredded coconut, although for quality and convenience canned milk cannot be faulted. If you need fresh coconut for a recipe, select one that sounds full of juice when it is shaken. (This juice is pleasant to drink, so if you wish to save it, either pierce one of the "eyes" of the coconut and drain it off or open the coconut carefully and collect the juice in a bowl.) To open a coconut, hold it in your left hand (if you are left-handed, hold in your right hand). Make sure the "eyes" are just above your thumb, then, using the back of a cleaver, strike the top or crown of the coconut. The coconut will fall apart easily after a few blows. Alternatively, place on a hard surface and hit with a hammer twice on the crown for the same effect.

Coconut juice: The liquid inside the coconut when it is shaken is coconut juice, not coconut milk. It is a refreshing drink but it is a bit of a performance to catch it. It is also made into palm wine, which can be quite potent.

Freshly grated coconut: When a little water is added, the coconut milk can be squeezed out by hand.

Canned coconut milk: This is available in 400ml/14fl oz/ 1⅔ cup cans, which come mostly from Thailand. It is more expensive to buy this ready-prepared product, but it is much more convenient and of excellent quality.

Instant powdered coconut: Instructions on the package show how to make cream, rich milk or milk according to how much water you add. The great advantage is that you can quickly make very small quantities as required.

Desiccated/dried shredded coconut: This is a very successful and inexpensive way of making good-quality coconut milk and cream, though it is labour intensive. Empty a 225g/8oz package of desiccated/dried shredded coconut into a food processor and pour over 425ml/15fl oz/1¾ cups boiling water. Process for 20–30 seconds and allow to cool a little. If making several batches, empty each quantity into a large bowl after processing and leave to cool. Place a sieve/fine-mesh strainer lined with muslin cloth/cheesecloth over a large bowl. Ladle some of the coconut into the muslin and fold the edges over, then twist the ends to squeeze out the maximum amount of milk. Repeat with the remaining coconut and discard the spent coconut each time. (You can use it to make a second batch, but it will be of poorer quality and should be used only to extend a good-quality first squeezing.) The cream will float to the top of the milk , so after 10 minutes you can scoop off the cream to use in a recipe as directed. Any leftover milk or cream can be stored in the refrigerator for a day, or longer in the freezer.

Creamed coconut: This is sold in 200g/7oz blocks, which must be kept in the refrigerator. Small slices can be added at the end of cooking curries or as instructed on the package.

CORIANDER OR CILANTRO
Ideally, buy a bunch of coriander/cilantro, roots and all. Keep in a plastic bag secured with an elastic band in the salad drawer in the refrigerator. The leaves are used all over Southeast Asia in salads and as a garnish, but the Thais also pound the stalks and roots to give an extra dimension to their curries, especially the renowned green variety. It has a distinctive pungent smell that complements a multitude of dishes. A coriander stem in the recipes denotes a single-rooted plant that has several stalks. Many bunches are sadly sold without the root, so use 4–5 stems as an equivalent.

CORIANDER SEEDS
These tiny, ball-shaped, beige-coloured seeds disguise their potential as one of the most highly regarded spices in Thai cookery. For the full impact, fry over a gentle heat without using any oil for a few minutes, either shaking the frying pan or stirring the seeds until they start to give off a spicy aroma. Grind to a fine powder and savour the heady perfume. It's magic, and it will discourage you from buying ready-ground coriander ever again!

CUMIN SEEDS
These scented seeds are frequently used with coriander seeds as a blend of spices. The two are used in garam masala and in many fish, chicken and meat curries and also pastes. The seeds look rather like hay seeds and should not be confused with fennel seeds, which are larger and have an aniseed flavour. Dry-fry and grind to a powder for the best results.

CURRY PASTES

There is a great deal of satisfaction to be had in making your own curry paste from scratch. You will need a rather large quantity of fresh chillies, so rubber gloves are a good idea if you are making several of the pastes in one go. Remember to scrape out the seeds from the chillies under running water so that the oils don't get in your eyes, and use a food processor to make the spicy ingredients into a first-class paste using the recipes on pages 24–5 . In Thailand the pastes are often made by hand, which results in a smoother consistency, but the prepared pastes available at markets and in some supermarkets are perfectly acceptable.

Make up at least the quantity given in the recipe, and store the remainder in the refrigerator in a glass jar (plastic containers retain the strong smells), labelled with the number of tablespoons in the jar. It will keep for several weeks in the refrigerator. Alternatively, freeze two tbsp at a time in cling film/plastic wrap, overwrapped with foil.

There are many ready-made curry pastes on the market, some of very good quality, which will cut down on the preparation time. Try out several before you find one that suits you. They are available in small sachets, 90g/3¼oz jars or up to 400g/14oz tubs, which are economical if Thai cookery has caught your imagination. The different curry pastes you might find are: red curry paste (*krueng gaeng phed*), green curry paste (*gaeng khiew waan*), jungle curry paste or country style (*gaeng pah*).

FERMENTED HOT AND SOUR MUSTARD GREENS

Fiery and hot as the name suggests, this vegetable is drained and finely chopped for use as an accompaniment to Chiang Mai Curried Noodle Soup with Chicken Khao (see page 70). A milder version, also sold in 140g/5oz cans, is fermented lettuce with chilli served in the same way. Either can be added to a stir-fry to add a little zip.

FISH SAUCE

Also known as *nam pla* in Thailand, fish sauce is widely used for flavouring. It is made throughout Southeast Asia, with each nationality claiming that its brand is best. It is made by packing anchovies into barrels with salt; the liquid that is eventually collected is the fish sauce. It is strong in flavour, fishy and salty, as you would expect, and is used to accentuate and complement other flavours. It is easy to come by and keeps very well in a cool place.

GALANGAL (KHA)

This member of the ginger family can sometimes be bought fresh from oriental stores. It is creamy coloured with rings on the skin, and if you are lucky enough to buy young galangal it may even have pink buds. The stems are straighter than the knobbly ones of ginger. To prepare, trim off the size you require, then peel and slice before using. The flesh is much more woody and fibrous than ginger, and has a pine-like smell. It is an essential ingredient in the famous *tom yum goong* – Thailand's best loved soup (see page 73). Store wrapped in newspaper in the bottom of the refrigerator, where it will keep for two weeks or more. Dried galangal powder (*laos*) can be bought; use one teaspoon for each 1cm/½in used in the recipe, though it is not nearly as good as the real thing.

GARLIC

This is used all over the region in very substantial quantities. The whole garlic is called a "bulb" and each segment a "clove". Choose plump-looking bulbs and store in a cool place. Many recipes require crushed garlic and for this you can use a garlic press or a pestle and mortar. Simply trim away the root before crushing.

GINGER

Young ginger, with its pale, creamy root, delicate pink nodules and green tips, can be bought all over Southeast Asia. It is used finely chopped in many stir-fry and fish dishes, but does not impart the pungent, aromatic flavour of the older, silvery-brown-skinned type that is readily available. Young ginger forms the basis for the exquisitely carved fish, birds and flowers in Thai cuisine. The older type, known as a hand, must be either peeled or scraped, then sliced and either chopped or pounded before being used.

Bruised ginger is suggested in some recipes. To bruise it, peel or scrape, then give a sharp blow with the end of a rolling pin or using a pestle and mortar. It will release its juices during cooking and can be removed from the dish before serving. Wrap in newspaper and store in the refrigerator salad drawer. See also galangal and krachai.

KAPI

An essential ingredient in the cooking of Southeast Asia, kapi is made from shrimp or prawns and salt, which are allowed to ferment then pounded into a fine paste. Dull pink to dark brown, fermented shrimp paste is generally sold in 225g/8oz blocks, although the Thai variety is available in 50g/2oz plastic containers. It keeps very well once opened if you rewrap it closely and store in an airtight container in a cool place. It has an unforgettable smell on first acquaintance but, strangely enough, does not dominate other flavours, rather adding depth and pungency, which are so much a part of the foods of the region. Where a recipe specifies 1cm/½in kapi, interpret this as a cube and prepare as follows. Either mould the kapi onto the end of a skewer and rotate over a low-to-medium gas flame or under the grill/broiler of an electric cooker/stove, until the outside begins to look crusty but not burned. Alternatively, to avoid such a strong smell, wrap in foil and place in a dry frying pan over a low heat for 5 minutes, turning from time to time. This takes away the rawness from the kapi and is essential when it is to be included in, say, a dressing or *nam prik*. If it is to be fried with other spices, this preliminary cooking may be omitted.

KRACHAI

The third member of the ginger family looks like a bunch of fingers. These are sliced diagonally and added to curries such as the Jungle Curry on page 101, where they give an earthy element to the dish. Store as for ginger and kapi.

LEMON GRASS

Fresh lemon grass stems are available in oriental stores, good-quality grocery store and some supermarkets. Huge clumps of this grass grow freely in warm climates. The long, slender leaves can be used to make a tea infusion, but the tightly packed stem, which is sometimes likened to a rather flat spring onion/scallion, is used for its wondrous lemony aroma and flavour. To prepare, cut off the root end and discard, then trim off the lower 6cm/2½in piece. This is sliced and sometimes pounded according to the recipe. Even as you cut the stem, just smell the marvellous lemon aroma. The top end of the stem can be either bruised and added to a curry for extra flavour (remove before serving if you like), or it can be bruised to make a brush with which to baste the meats on satay sticks with a little oil as they cook, or to stir a sauce (see page 31). This is another illustration of the resourcefulness of Southeast Asian cooks: nothing is discarded. See also Thai Fish Cakes on page 46 for a clever way of using lemon grass stems.

Lemon grass will keep well for two to three weeks if closely wrapped in newspaper and placed in the vegetable box of the refrigerator. For longer-term storage, prepare as directed above, then place the pounded, fleshy part in a plastic box in the freezer, making a note of how many stems have been pounded. When firm, mark into sections of, say, two stems per portion for future use. The top part of the stems can be wrapped closely and frozen too. Freeze-dried lemon grass is also available in jars from good supermarkets, which can be used instead: use one teaspoon for each stem. Some books suggest a strip of lemon zest, but this is no substitute for the real thing.

LIME LEAVES (MAGRUT)

Known as *bai magrut*, these leaves really catch the eye: they are dark green and glossy with a "waist". They come from the kaffir lime tree, and are used widely in Thai cuisine. They are torn or finely shredded, then added to an enormous range of dishes from soups to curries, contributing a unique lime/lemon flavour. For long-term storage, wrap washed leaves and store in the freezer. No thawing is required before use, which makes this a very convenient way of storing them. (Freeze-dried kaffir lime leaves are now available in jars from major supermarkets.) If you cannot get hold of lime leaves, use grated grapefruit zest as a substitute.

The fruit, known as the kaffir lime, or magrut, resembles a rather gnarled lemon. Only the zest is used in recipes, finely grated, though a dried variety is available. It must be soaked before use.

MANGO

Green mangoes are very popular in salads (see page 97). To prepare a ripe mango, see page 178.

NOODLES

Egg noodles: Referred to as *bah mee*, these rich yellow noodles are available fresh or frozen from oriental stores and supermarkets. If not frozen, use within two days. Either allow to thaw at room temperature or plunge into boiling water briefly until soft, stirring often, then drain and use as directed. Dried egg noodles are also available: soak for 10 minutes before cooking in salted, boiling water for 2 minutes until tender, or follow the package directions.

Rice noodles: Known as *guay tiew*, these can be bought fresh from some oriental stores. The wide strips, which are folded sometimes and look like cannelloni, contain flecks of dried prawn/shrimp or spring onions/scallions. Plunge into boiling water. Drain, then cut the still-folded noodles into narrow strips and use in stir-fries. Keep covered before cooking to prevent the noodles drying out.

Flat dried rice noodles: These come in three widths and are referred to as *sen mei* (3mm/⅛in), *sen lek* (5mm/¼in) and *sen yai* (7–8mm/⅜in). Soak in warm water for 15 minutes if required quickly or place in cold water and leave until you are ready to cook. Drain and use in stir-fries or soups.

Rice vermicelli: These thin round noodles are deep-fried for *mee krob* (see page 149) or soaked in warm water for 1–2 minutes before being drained and used in soups or stir-fries.

Bean thread noodles: These are made from mung beans and they resemble nylon fishing line gathered up into a skein. Soak them in warm water for 10 minutes before draining and cutting them into short lengths with scissors. Use in appetizers such as Thai Spring Rolls (see page 42) and Money Bags (see page 54) or add to soups.

OYSTER SAUCE

Made from an extract of oysters, soy sauce, salt and starches, oyster sauce gives a characteristic flavour to meat dishes and vegetables in particular. It keeps well but you may need to add a little boiling water if it thickens up as you reach the end of the bottle.

PANDANUS LEAF

This resembles a gladiolius leaf, and is a very popular addition to rice dishes and desserts, to which it imparts a warm flavour. It is also wonderful in plain boiled or steamed rice. For the maximum flavour, hold the leaf at one end and pull the prongs of a fork through it, then tie it in a knot and add to the recipe as directed (see Coconut Rice on page 30). It is available fresh from oriental stores; keep any extra leaves in the freezer.

PEANUTS OR GROUNDNUTS

The name "groundnuts" is apt, because these nuts are dug from the ground at harvest time, often by hand. The nuts are highly nutritious, with a 30 per cent protein content and a 40–50 per cent oil content. They are used widely all over the region in many dishes, sauces and for garnishing. If salted peanuts are used instead, be sure to taste before adding extra salt. Crunchy peanut butter is an alternative to crushed and pounded peanuts in the sauces in this book. Peanut or groundnut oil is popular for cooking and widely available. Roast raw peanuts in a wok without oil, turning for about 8 minutes until golden. Cool and store.

PEPPERCORNS

These grow on a vine, which is trained up a tripod-shaped structure. The berries grow in clusters like tiny grapes, are harvested when ripe and then dried in the sun on large mats, where they are turned regularly and become black peppercorns. For white peppercorns, the berries are soaked in running water for a week to rot the hard casing, then rubbed by hand to remove this completely before being sun-dried.

PORK CRACKLING

Also known as chicaron, this is made from pork rind that has been deep-fried, forming puffy, crisp crackers. It is sold in oriental stores and is served as the crunchy element alongside curries, sliced in salads or with Nam Prik Sauce (see page 50).

PRAWN CRACKERS OR SHRIMP CHIPS

These have become universally popular not only as an accompaniment to Southeast Asian food but also as a snack. They are sold in 225g/8oz packages, which should be stored in a cool, dry place. To cook, follow the instructions on page 53. Store any leftovers in an airtight container, though this is rarely necessary as they are so moreish.

PRAWNS OR SHRIMP

The dried varieties are sun-dried and have a long shelf life. They are usually sold in packages and need to be soaked in water and drained before being used whole or chopped in soups or with vegetables. In some recipes dried prawns/shrimp are pounded to make a powder using a pestle and mortar. Make up a quantity if making many Thai dishes. Powdered prawns/shrimp are also sold in packages.

PRESERVED PLUMS

These add a sharp, salty taste (see the sauce on page 154). They are sold in jars, and any leftovers will keep in the refrigerator. Do not discard the clear liquid.

RICE

This is a staple food for two-thirds of the world's population. Thai fragrant long-grain rice is widely available and has a reputation for quality and perfume. Many homes where a lot of rice is consumed have a rice cooker (see page 21).

RICE WINE VINEGAR

This is a mild vinegar. You could use white wine or cider vinegar instead.

SESAME SEEDS

After India and China, Myanmar is the third largest producer of sesame seeds. The whole plant is cut at harvest time and stacked upright until the seed pods begin to burst open, releasing the tiny seeds. The seeds are widely used in oriental cooking, either dry-fried or toasted to extract their delicious nutty flavour. Two other products come from the seeds: tahini, which is a crushed sesame paste, and sesame oil. The seeds are rich in oil (45–50 per cent). The oil is not used for frying as it has a low burning temperature but it is often used to dress vegetables just before serving.

SHALLOTS

These mild members of the onion family are widely used, but if you cannot buy them, substitute one red onion for six to eight shallot segments. (This will give a much deeper colour to your finished dish.) Alternatively, use a brown-skinned Spanish-type onion.

SOY SAUCE

This is an indispensable ingredient in the cooking of Southeast Asia. Each country uses a light (thin) and a dark (thick) soy sauce. The sauce is made from fermented soybeans, wheat grain, salt and water. Light soy sauce is the most widely used. Dark, or black, soy sauce is much thicker and darker in colour, so add with care. It also has a sugar content, unlike the thin sauce. Mushroom-flavoured dark soy sauce imparts a lot of depth in flavouring.

SQUID

Ready-cleaned squid can be easily bought either fresh or frozen from larger supermarkets. If frozen, thaw, then pull the tentacles from each pocket when sufficiently thawed. Slit down the side of the pocket and open it out. Score the inner surface lightly with the back of a knife and cut each one into two or three strips. They will curl obligingly in the hot wok, as will the tentacles, and the scoring helps the sauce to permeate the flesh. These curls look so pretty, but you can save time by simply cutting the squid into rings.

STRAW MUSHROOMS

Sold in cans, these are an attractive addition to many fish, vegetable and stir-fry recipes. They are grown in straw, as the name suggests. If you cannot find them, use button mushrooms instead.

STOCK

A really good fish or chicken stock will enhance the flavour of all your recipes (see page 23 for recipes), though you can use stock/bouillon cubes and water if needs be. Make the stock using fish bones, prawn/shrimp shells or a chicken carcass or a pack of chicken wings. I often buy a whole chicken, use the leg and breast meat for a recipe and then use the carcass to make stock to freeze in 300ml/10½fl oz/1¼ cup quantities. Remember to label before freezing, as all stocks look the same out of the freezer. If you have square plastic boxes (a good shape for storing in the freezer), label a plastic bag, place it in a box, then fill. When the stock is frozen, you can remove the stock in the bag from the box, tie up the top and return it to the freezer until required.

TAMARIND

This is used to add tartness to recipes all over the region, just as we might use vinegar or lemon juice. The tamarind tree is a magnificent specimen that produces large pods about the size of a broad/fava bean pod. They are sold loose, but the more usual way is to buy the purée from the pod in a 225g/8oz block, which looks like a block of dates. It keeps for a long time if closely wrapped in a cool place.

To make tamarind juice, mix one teaspoon of tamarind pulp with a few tablespoons of warm water. Leave to stand for 10 minutes, then mix by hand to release the pulp from the seeds. Strain through a sieve/fine-mesh strainer and discard the pulp and seeds; the resulting water is ready to be used in a recipe. Tamarind purée is even easier: use one tablespoon to four tablespoons of water. A ready-made juice is also available.

Dried tamarind looks rather like dried apple slices. It also needs to be soaked (use two slices in water just to cover), but as it is dry you need to allow 30 minutes to extract the maximum flavour, then strain and use the juice.

WATER CHESTNUTS

Canned water chestnuts are used for their crisp, crunchy texture. Any leftovers can be added to a fruit salad or used in Thai Rubies in Sweetened Coconut Milk (see page 186).

WING BEANS

These unusual-looking light green beans have a type of frill down four sides. This attractive feature is shown to advantage when the beans are sliced diagonally before cooking. Choose the smaller ones for crispness – they are tougher when older. Use them in stir-fries (see page 121) and salads or blanch before serving with Nam Prik Sauce (see page 50). If unavailable, use green beans instead.

WRAPPERS

Spring/egg roll and wonton wrappers come in square and round shapes and in different sizes. They are usually found in the freezer section of an oriental store. Allow them to thaw, then, when ready for use, open the pack and carefully tease up one corner from the pile and peel away. Repeat until all the wrappers have been placed in a pile. Cover with a damp cloth to prevent drying out before filling.

EQUIPMENT

BARBECUE

Some recipes, such as satay dishes, gain extra flavour by being cooked over charcoal. A gas or electric grill/broiler can be used, but charcoal does add to the flavour, and is essential if you want to cook and eat a Thai meal outdoors.

CLEAVER

This multi-purpose, heavy, broad-bladed implement is used with great skill by oriental cooks for chopping, slicing, mincing/grinding or even crushing garlic by pressing down on the broad side of the blade. Buy one and try it out.

PESTLE AND MORTAR/FOOD PROCESSOR

The pestle and mortar and/or food processor feature a great deal in the making of spice pastes and the pounding and blending of ingredients.

The traditional granite pestle and mortar is quite deep and is pitted, which makes it ideal for grinding and pounding wet spices. Chilli, garlic, galangal, ginger and lemon grass are held by the rough surface and do not fly out while being pounded, though the ingredients should be sliced before pounding for the best results. For grinding or pounding small quantities of wet or dry spices, this type of pestle and mortar is ideal.

If using a food processor, slice fibrous ingredients such as galangal, ginger and lemon grass before processing and, if a particularly fine, smooth paste is required, bruise them

first using the pestle and mortar. If you add oil to the spice paste ingredients to ease the blending, do remember to reduce the amount of oil for frying to compensate for this.

RICE COOKER

If you eat a lot of rice and want a foolproof method of achieving perfect results every time, plus rice that is kept warm until you need it, then a rice cooker is ideal.

STEAMERS

Bamboo, stacking-type steamers are widely available. They are multi-purpose in that they can be used for serving as well as cooking the food.

WOK

This wide, circular pan with a curved base not only enables you to cook a large quantity of food simultaneously over a large surface but also allows for the rapid evaporation of liquid, which is essential in many recipes. It is the ideal shape for tossing food in stir-fry recipes, is a much more satisfactory shape than a frying pan for deep-frying and can also be used for steaming. Buy the heaviest one you can find, as the thin, lightweight woks will burn food very easily. If you have a gas cooker/stove, you will need to use a metal stand for the wok. A useful tip: warm the wok over a gentle heat before adding the oil, which then floods over the heated surface more easily and prevents food sticking.

COOKING METHODS

BARBECUING

Charcoal is used extensively for cooking throughout Southeast Asia. Where this is not feasible, use the grill/broiler for satay, for example, or roast in the oven if portions of spare ribs or chicken are used (see pages 166 and 169).

DEEP-FRYING

The wok is ideal for deep-frying, requiring less oil than conventional deep-frying saucepans yet providing a larger surface area for cooking. Use a thermometer to keep an eye on the temperature, if possible.

STEAMING

The beauty of bamboo baskets stacked neatly on top of each other is that they give great versatility: you can use just one basket or several over the same wok. Do not fill the baskets too full, or the steam will not penetrate evenly. Aluminium Chinese-style steamers are sold in Chinese stores and usually consist of two perforated trays with a lid to sit above a saucepan. When steaming, always have a kettle of boiling water ready to fill up the wok, steamer base or saucepan. The Thais are very keen on using banana leaf parcels for steaming whole fish (see Steamed Whole Fish with Preserved Plums in Banana Leaf Parcel on page 154).

When small items are being cooked, line each basket with a piece of damp muslin/cheesecloth. You can then stack them one on top of the other with the lid set on top before setting them over the wok, replenishing the boiling water as needed. If you have a metal trivet that sits in the wok over the water, you can cook a whole fish. Cover with a lid and keep an eye on the water level while steaming.

Finally, a two-tier electric steamer is a real boon when the top of the cooker/stove is being used for curries and stir-fry dishes and there is no space for a steamer.

STIR-FRYING

No matter what is being cooked, all the ingredients must be ready before you start cooking, as the whole process is essentially fast in order to retain maximum flavour, colour and crispness, especially when cooking vegetables.

When all the ingredients are ready, warm the wok over a gentle flame, then pour in the oil and swirl it around before adding the first ingredients, be it spice paste or chopped onion, garlic and ginger. (You will need much less oil for stir-frying than for conventional frying, which is a plus point from the health point of view.) When stir-frying, you must keep everything on the move all the time to ensure even cooking. The reason for adding ingredients at high temperatures is to seal in the juices of the finely chopped ingredients, so retaining all the flavour. Some vegetables, such as broccoli, should be quickly plunged into boiling water (this is known as blanching), then drained and rinsed with cold water to retain their bright green colour, before being added to the stir-fry dish.

STOCKS

Fish or Chicken Stock
Nahm Sup Goong or *Nahm Sup Gai*

Makes 1 litre/35fl oz/4¼ cups • Preparation time: 10 minutes
• Cooking time: 35 minutes

450g/1lb fish bones from sole, plaice or other white fish
    or 1 chicken carcass, broken into pieces, or 1 pack chicken
    wings
1 onion, quartered
2.5cm/1in piece fresh root ginger, bruised
1 lemon grass stem, bruised
1 lime leaf (optional)
6 coriander/cilantro stems, stalks and roots
    bruised (optional)
salt and freshly ground black pepper

1 **WASH** the fish or raw chicken bones in cold water first.
    Place in a large saucepan and cover with 1.5 litres/52fl
    oz/6½ cups water.
2 **BRING** to the boil, then skim if necessary.
3 **ADD** the onion, ginger, lemon grass, lime leaf and
    coriander/cilantro, if using, and some seasoning. Return
    to the boil, turn the heat down and then simmer for
    20 minutes only, without a lid, for the fish stock or for
    30 minutes (half-covered) for the chicken stock. Remove
    from the heat.
4 **COOL**, then strain into a clean container. Use immediately
    or cool and chill or freeze in small quantities until required.

Vegetable Stock
Nahm Sup Pak

Makes 1.4 litres/48fl oz/6 cups • Preparation time:
10 minutes • Cooking time: 30–40 minutes

700g/1½lb (total weight) of the following vegetables:
    white cabbage, carrots, celery, leeks and onions
1 tsp salt and a little freshly ground black pepper
4 tsp light soy sauce
½ tsp sugar

1 **DISCARD** the outer leaves and the thick stalks from
    the piece of cabbage and shred finely. Chop the carrots,
    chop the celery stalks, slice the leeks and cut the onions
    into quarters.
2 **PLACE** the prepared vegetables in a large saucepan and
    cover with 2 litres/70fl oz/8½ cups water. Add the salt and
    pepper and bring to the boil. Reduce the heat, half-cover
    and simmer for 30–40 minutes until the vegetables are
    tender.
3 **STRAIN** the stock through a fine sieve/fine-mesh strainer
    and return it to the saucepan.
4 **BOIL** for a further 5 minutes without a lid. Stir in the soy
    sauce and sugar.
5 **COOL**, then use immediately or cool completely and chill or
    freeze in small quantities until required.

PASTES

Red Curry Paste
Krueng Gaeng Phed

Makes 375g/13oz/1½ cups • Preparation time:
30–35 minutes • Cooking time: 2–3 minutes

10 red chillies, deseeded and sliced
115g/4oz red onions or shallots, sliced
4 garlic cloves, sliced
3 lemon grass stems, lower stem only, sliced and bruised
1cm/½in piece galangal, peeled and sliced
4 coriander/cilantro stems, stalks and roots only
1–2 tbsp sunflower oil
1 tsp grated magrut
1cm/½in cube prepared kapi (see page 15)
1 tbsp coriander seeds
2 tsp cumin seeds
8–10 black peppercorns
1 tsp salt

1 **BLEND** the chillies, onions or shallots, garlic, lemon grass, galangal and coriander/cilantro to a fine paste with the oil in a food processor. Add the magrut and prepared kapi.

2 **DRY-FRY** the seeds for a few minutes, then grind to a powder with the peppercorns using a pestle and mortar. Add to the paste with the salt. Blend well. Spoon into a glass jar, cover with cling film/plastic wrap and a tight-fitting lid and refrigerate.

Green Curry Paste
Gaeng Khiew Waan

Makes 325g/11oz/1⅓ cups • Preparation time:
30–35 minutes • Cooking time: 2–3 minutes

10 green chillies, deseeded and sliced
115g/4oz white onions or shallots, sliced
4 garlic cloves, sliced
3 lemon grass stems, lower stem only, sliced and bruised
1cm/½in piece galangal, peeled and sliced
4 coriander/cilantro stems, leaves, stalks and roots
4 lime leaves, sliced
1–2 tbsp sunflower oil
1 tsp grated magrut
1cm/½in cube prepared kapi (see page 15)
1 tbsp coriander seeds
2 tsp cumin seeds
8–10 black peppercorns
1 tsp salt

1 **BLEND** the chillies, onions or shallots, garlic, lemon grass, galangal, coriander/cilantro and lime leaves to a fine paste with the oil in a food processor. Add the magrut and prepared kapi.

2 **DRY-FRY** the seeds for a few minutes, then grind to a powder with the peppercorns using a pestle and mortar. Add to the spice paste with the salt. Store as for red curry paste.

Mussaman Curry Paste
Gaeng Mussaman

Assemble and prepare the same ingredients as for the red curry paste, but follow the different preparation of the fresh ingredients. The frying greatly enhances the flavours before the mixture is processed into a paste.

Makes 280g/10oz/1¼ cups • Preparation time: 30–35 minutes • Cooking time: 5 minutes

red curry paste ingredients (see page 24)
6 cardamom pods
½ tsp ground cloves
½ tsp cinnamon

1 FRY the chillies with the onions, or shallots garlic, lemon grass and galangal in a little oil, stirring for 3 minutes over a low heat to bring out the flavours.

2 TURN into a food processor and blend the ingredients to a smooth paste. Add the coriander/cilantro stalks, magrut and kapi. Blend again.

3 FRY the coriander and cumin seeds in a dry frying pan for a few minutes with the cardamom pods and salt. Remove the seeds from the pods and pound to a powder with the black peppercorns using a pestle and mortar.

4 ADD the cloves and cinnamon, turn into a food processor with the spice paste and blend again until very smooth.

Hung Lay Curry Paste
Gaeng Hung Lay

Makes 250g/9oz/1 cup • Preparation time: 25 minutes

2.5cm/1in cube prepared kapi (see page 15)
10 dried red chillies, some or all of the seeds removed, torn into pieces
25–30g/1oz galangal, thinly peeled and sliced
2 lemon grass stems, lower 6cm/2½in trimmed and sliced, stems bruised
3 garlic cloves
3 large shallots, halved

1 PUT all the ingredients into a food processor and process until the paste is well blended.

2 TRANSFER to a screwtop glass jar with some cling film/ plastic wrap between the jar and lid. Refrigerate for up to 2 months.

Garnishes

Banana cups

1 **PLACE** a banana leaf on a large chopping/cutting board. Mark out discs using a 14cm/5½in saucer for the smaller-size cups or 17cm/7in plate to match larger ramekins.

2 **CUT** around the discs with a sharp knife and plunge into a bowl of boiling water.

3 **PLACE** 2 leaf discs together with the under sides facing and with the grain of each going in a different direction, which strengthens the cup shape.

4 **MAKE** a tuck at one point and staple firmly. Repeat with the opposite side and then at the other two corners to obtain a cup shape. These are shown with Khun Nan's Steamed Fish Curry on page 113.

Chilli flowers

1 **CHOOSE** a small, finger-length chilli and slit the top two-thirds of it into fine strips.

2 **LEAVE** it in cold, or even iced, water to speed up the curling operation, then scrape away the seeds, if wished.

Cucumber garnishes

1 **MAKE** a fan by cutting notches down each side of the skin of a 7.5cm/3in piece of cucumber, then slicing thinly toward the end without cutting right through.

2 **MAKE** a folded garnish by thinly slicing a 15cm/6in piece of cucumber almost through to the bottom, then folding it in alternate slices. (Thai cucumbers are fairly pliable.)

Spring onion curls

1 **CHOOSE** a finger-length piece of spring onion/scallion, firm green part only, and discard the root.

2 **HOLD** it in the centre and use a sharp knife to cut the stem into strips from the centre to the end in each direction.

3 **PLACE** in cold water to curl.

4 **CREATE** a variation by threading a slice of chilli onto the finger-length piece of stem in the middle and repeating the cutting as above.

Spring onion tassels

1 **CHOOSE** the white root part of a not-too-large spring onion/scallion that has a little green top to it.

2 **CUT** it to finger length and discard the root. Hold at the base and, using a sharp knife, cut the top two-thirds through and up to the top several times.

3 **PLACE** in cold water to curl. This makes a very attractive garnish for the centre of a dish.

Sauces

Dipping Sauces

The basic dipping sauce has a sugar syrup base with the addition of vinegar and salt. This underlines the three basic flavours in Thai food: sweet, sour and salty.

Makes 500ml/17fl oz/2 cups • Preparation time: 3–4 minutes • Cooking time: 8–9 minutes

450g/1lb/2 cups sugar
2 tbsp wine vinegar or rice vinegar
1½ tbsp salt

1 **HEAT** the sugar with 500ml/17fl oz/2 cups water in a saucepan, stirring until the sugar dissolves. Allow to boil for 4–5 minutes to become syrupy. Remove from the heat and add the vinegar and salt.

2 **RETURN** to the heat and boil for 2 minutes, then remove from the heat and cool. Divide as suggested below.

3 **POUR** half the prepared sugar syrup into a separate pan, and use this for the sweet chilli dipping sauce (see right).

4 **DIVIDE** the remaining syrup between two saucepans, and use these to make the preserved plum dipping sauce and dark soy dipping sauce (see right).

5 **ADD** each flavouring, then return to the boil, turn the heat down and simmer for a further 1 minute.

6 **COOL** and transfer to glass jars. If the syrup thickens too much, add a little boiling water and stir. Cover each jar with cling film/plastic wrap, then seal with a lid.

Sweet Chilli Dipping Sauce
Nam Prik Waan

Add 6 tbsp sweet chilli sauce to 300ml/10½fl oz/1¼ cups prepared sugar syrup.

Preserved Plum Dipping Sauce
Nam Bouy

Add 3–4 finely chopped preserved plums to 100ml/3½fl oz/scant ½ cup prepared sugar syrup.

Dark Soy Dipping Sauce
Si-Ew Waan

Add 1 tbsp dark soy sauce to 100ml/3½fl oz/scant ½ cup prepared sugar syrup.

Peanut Sauce

Nam Jeem Satay

Delicious morsels of barbecued meats or prawns/shrimp on bamboo or wooden skewers are complemented by this famous peanut sauce.

Makes 450ml/16fl oz/scant 2 cups • Preparation time: 15 minutes • Cooking time: 8–10 minutes

2 tsp tamarind pulp
1 can coconut milk (400ml/14fl oz/1²/₃ cups)
1–2 tsp Mussaman curry paste (see page 25)
2 tbsp dark brown sugar
1–2 tsp fish sauce
85–115g/3–4oz/½–¾ cup roasted peanuts, coarsely ground, or crunchy peanut butter

1 **SOAK** the tamarind pulp in 2 tbsp warm water for 10 minutes, then strain (see page 20). Meanwhile, pour one-third of the coconut milk into a wok or saucepan and heat through until bubbling.

2 **ADD** the curry paste and cook gently for 2–3 minutes, stirring all the time to bring out the full flavour.

3 **ADD** the sugar, remaining coconut milk, strained tamarind and fish sauce to taste. Allow to bubble to thicken the mixture slightly, then add the peanuts or peanut butter.

4 **CONTINUE** cooking, stirring, for a few minutes until the sauce has a creamy consistency. Taste and adjust the seasoning by adding more fish sauce if necessary.

Thai Relish

Makes 100ml/3½fl oz/scant ½ cup • Preparation time: 8 minutes • Serve this relish with a variety of snacks and appetizers.

1–2 red chillies, deseeded and finely sliced
2.5cm/1in piece cucumber, halved, deseeded, and finely chopped
1 coriander/cilantro stem
1 shallot or ½ small red onion, very finely sliced
3 tbsp basic dipping sauce or sweet chilli dipping sauce (see page 27)

1 **PLACE** the chillies, cucumber, chopped stalk of the coriander/cilantro, shallot or red onion and dipping sauce in a serving bowl.

2 **USE** a little chilli and the coriander leaves, lightly chopped, for a garnish.

Alternative to using dipping sauce:

1 tbsp sugar
2 tbsp cider vinegar
1 tsp fish sauce

1 **STIR** the sugar and vinegar together until the sugar has dissolved. Just before serving, pour this sauce over the chopped ingredients. Taste for seasoning and add fish sauce as required.

2 **GARNISH** as before.

BASIC RECIPES

Plain Boiled Rice
Khao Tom

Serves 4 • Preparation time: 2 minutes • Cooking time: 12–15 minutes

1 **WASH** 225g/8oz/1 cup rice in several changes of water until the water looks clear, to remove the starch.
2 **PLACE** the rice in a heavy saucepan with 500ml/ 17fl oz/2 cups water and bring to the boil. Reduce the heat, stir, cover the pan and simmer for 12–15 minutes.
3 **REMOVE** the lid and stir with a chopstick or fork.
4 **USE** at once or transfer to a serving bowl, three-quarters covered with cling film/plastic wrap, and microwave on full power for 4 minutes in 650w microwave or 3 minutes in 900w just before serving. Alternatively, place in an oiled steamer, cover with a lid and set over a saucepan of gently bubbling water for 8–10 minutes until well heated. Stir with a chopstick to avoid breaking up the grains.

Microwaved Rice

Serves 4 • Preparation time: 2 minutes • Cooking time: 12–15 minutes

1 **WASH** 225g/8oz/1 cup rice thoroughly as for boiled rice.
2 **COOK** the rice in 425ml/¾ pint/1¾ cups boiling water in a bowl three-quarters covered with cling film/plastic wrap for 10 minutes on full power, then rest for 5 minutes in the microwave. (For easy-cook rice, follow the package directions.)
3 **REMOVE** and stir as for boiled rice.

Glutinous Rice
Khao Niaw

Available in black and white, this rice is very starchy, hence the common name "sticky rice". It can be gathered up into a ball with the fingers, then dipped into curries and other dishes. All over Thailand the white variety is cooked with coconut milk and served with fresh mango slices (see page 174).

Serves 4 • Overnight soaking time • Cooking time: 25 minutes

1 **SOAK** 225g/8oz/1 cup glutinous rice overnight in water to cover, then drain and rinse.
2 **TURN** into a muslin cloth/cheesecloth-lined colander or steamer and place over gently bubbling water for about 25 minutes (longer the soaking, the shorter the cooking).
3 **TASTE** to check whether the rice is cooked: it should be just tender with a little resistance.

Steamed Rice
Khao Suay

Serves 3–4 • Preparation time: 3 minutes
• Cooking time: 25 minutes

225g/8oz/1 cup Thai fragrant rice
½ tsp salt
oil, for brushing

1 **PLACE** the rice in a sieve/fine-mesh strainer or a bowl and
   rinse thoroughly.
2 **BRING** 600ml/21fl oz/2½ cups water to a boil in a heavy
   saucepan. Stir in the rice and salt. Return to the boil and stir
   once or twice to prevent the rice settling on the pan bottom.
   Cook uncovered over a medium heat for 6–8 minutes until
   the water has been absorbed and the surface is covered in
   tiny crater-like holes.
3 **BRUSH** the base of the steamer lightly with oil. If it has
   large holes, cover with either a muslin cloth/cheesecloth or
   some foil that has been punctured with several holes to
   allow the steam to cook the rice. Drain the rice in a sieve/
   strainer or colander.
4 **TRANSFER** the rice into the steamer; make a few holes in
   the rice with a chopstick so that the steam can circulate. Set
   the steamer over a saucepan of boiling water. Cover with the
   lid and allow to cook for 15 minutes, when the rice will be
   fluffy and ready to serve. Top up with boiling water as needed.
5 **FORK** through with a roasting fork or chopstick. The rice
   can be cooked an hour or more ahead of the meal and
   reheated as for boiled rice (see page 29).

Coconut Rice
Hung Khao Man

This is a favourite accompaniment for market salad (see
page 94). If you live near a Thai store, look out for fresh
pandanus leaves, which add a really special flavour.

Serves 3–4 • Preparation time: 2 minutes
• Cooking time: 20 minutes

225g/8oz/1 cup Thai fragrant rice
225ml/8fl oz/scant 1 cup coconut milk
1 prepared pandanus leaf (see page 17)
½ tsp salt
1 tbsp sugar

1 **WASH** the rice thoroughly in several changes of
   cold water.
2 **PLACE** the coconut milk and in a heavy saucepan with
   125ml/4fl oz/½ cup water, and bring to the boil.
   Add the rice, pandanus leaf, salt and sugar and return
   to the boil.
3 **REDUCE** the heat, cover with a lid and cook gently
   for 15 minutes, or until the rice is tender.
4 **LEAVE** in the covered saucepan for a further 5 minutes
   before serving. Fork through with a roasting fork so that the
   grains remain whole and separate.
5 **REMOVE** the pandanus leaf before serving.

Rice Salad
Khao Yum

A typically Southern Thai creation of fragrant rice piled in the centre of a large serving dish, surrounded by neat piles of beautifully prepared raw vegetables, spices and peanuts, then topped with a drizzle of fresh chilli and lemon or lime juice dressing. It's a marvellous way to use up leftover rice as a quick lunch dish. You can prepare it ahead of time, putting the salad ingredients into covered containers in the refrigerator until required.

Serves 4, or more as side dish • Preparation time: 25 minutes

115g/4oz long or green beans, cut into 2.5cm/1in lengths
3 lemon grass stems, lower 6cm/2½in removed and
   shredded, tops bruised
3 carrots, coarsely grated
150g/5½oz firm white cabbage, very finely sliced or grated
1 bunch spring onions/scallions, very finely shredded
2–3 lime leaves, finely shredded
5cm/2in piece fresh root ginger, peeled and cut
   into matchsticks
115g/4oz/generous 1 cup bean sprouts
115g/4oz/¾ cup roasted peanuts
225g/8oz/1 cup Thai fragrant rice, cooked and left to go cold
1 handful sweet basil and coriander/cilantro leaves, to
   garnish

FOR THE DRESSING
3–4 red chillies
juice of 2 lemons or limes
3–4 tbsp fish sauce
1 tsp sugar

1 PLUNGE the beans into boiling water, then drain them, rinse with cold water and drain again. (This process, called blanching, turns the beans a bright shade of green.)

2 ARRANGE all the ingredients in neat piles on one or two large serving dishes with the rice in the centre not too long before the salad is to be eaten.

3 GARNISH the salad attractively with the basil and coriander/cilantro leaves.

4 MAKE the dressing. Pound the chillies using a pestle and mortar, with or without the seeds depending on how hot you like your food. (If unsure, err on the side of caution: you can always add some seeds later but you can't take them away.)

5 ADD the lemon or lime juice and fish sauce little by little, tasting as you go, until it suits your taste, adding some sugar if necessary to balance the flavours. Pour into a gravy boat and stir with the bruised lemon grass stems.

6 PLACE the dish of rice salad in the centre of the table with the gravy boat to one side. Serve, with guests taking a little of each ingredient and drizzling some of the dressing on top. Each person then tosses their salad together lightly before eating.

Thai Fried Rice
Khao Pad

A stunning blend of Thai fragrant rice, cooked chicken or pork, prawns/shrimp and vegetables, pepped-up with red curry paste, sensitively seasoned and garnished with omelette strips and lemon or lime wedges. Like Thai fried noodles, this is almost a meal in itself and takes no time to put together if the rice is already cooked and cold.

Serves 4 • Preparation time: 20 minutes
• Cooking time: 8–10 minutes

800g/1lb 12oz/5 cups cold cooked Thai fragrant rice
   (345g/12oz/1½ cups dry weight)
4 tbsp sunflower oil
2 eggs, beaten with 2 tbsp water, lightly seasoned
1 tbsp red curry paste (see page 24)
175g/6oz chicken breast or boneless pork fillet, very
   thinly sliced
1 onion, finely sliced
1 handful green beans, trimmed into short lengths
1 can sweetcorn (200g/7oz/scant 1 cup), drained
1 tbsp fish sauce
1 tsp sugar
175g/6oz shelled cooked prawns/shrimp
4 spring onions/scallions, trimmed and shredded
1 small handful coriander/cilantro leaves, to garnish
1 lemon or lime, cut into fine wedges, to serve

1 **STIR** the cooked rice with chopsticks or the prongs of a roasting fork to loosen the grains.

2 **HEAT** 1 tbsp of the oil in a frying pan and make 2 thin omelettes from the egg mixture. Cook on one side only, then roll up tightly. When cold, cut into slices.

3 **HEAT** a wok and add the remaining oil. Add the curry paste, then add the chicken or pork slices and toss all the time until they change colour and are tender.

4 **ADD** the onion slices, then the beans, and continue cooking over a fairly high heat, tossing all the time.

5 **ADD** the sweetcorn, rice, fish sauce, sugar, prawns/shrimp and some of the spring onions/scallions. Taste for seasoning. When very hot, turn onto a hot serving dish or serve from the wok.

6 **GARNISH** with the omelette slices, remaining spring onions and coriander/cilantro leaves and serve with the lemon or lime wedges.

Thai Fried Noodles
Kuay Tiaw Pad Thai

**Serves 4–5 • Preparation time: 20–25 minutes
• Cooking time: 12 minutes**

450g/1lb flat dried rice noodles
1 tsp tamarind pulp
4–5 tbsp sunflower oil
2 eggs, beaten with 2 tbsp water
salt and freshly ground black pepper
3 shallots or 1 red onion, roughly chopped
2 garlic cloves
2 dried chillies, deseeded if liked
115g/4oz fresh bean curd, cut into cubes (optional)
1 tbsp dark brown sugar
1–2 tbsp fish sauce
225g/8oz shelled cooked prawns/shrimp
175g/6oz/2 cups bean sprouts
2 tbsp dried powdered prawns/shrimp
25g/1oz/scant ¼ cup peanuts, crushed
6 cubes deep-fried bean curd
1 red chilli, deseeded and shredded, to garnish
1 small handful coriander/cilantro leaves, to garnish
½ bunch spring onions/scallions, shredded, to garnish
1 lime or lemon, cut into wedges, to serve

1 **COVER** the noodles with warm water to soften for about
   10 minutes before needed. Drain and cover with a clean
   damp cloth.
2 **SOAK** the tamarind pulp in 2 tbsp warm water for
   10 minutes, then strain (see page 20).

3 **HEAT** a frying pan and add 2 tbsp of the oil. Season the
   beaten eggs and make 2 very thin omelettes, cooking
   on one side only. Roll one into a sausage shape and cut
   into thin slices when cold. Leave the other whole.
4 **POUND** the shallots or red onion, garlic and dried chillies
   to a paste using a pestle and mortar or food processor.
   Heat the remaining oil in a wok and fry the paste without
   browning. Add the fresh bean curd cubes, if using. Stir in
   the brown sugar, tamarind juice and fish sauce to taste.
5 **ADD** the softened noodles and toss well, adding a little
   water if necessary to keep the noodles moist. Add the
   prawns/shrimp and cook over a high heat for 1 minute.
6 **ADD** the omelette strips and most of the bean sprouts,
   remove from the heat and adjust the seasoning if necessary.
7 **PILE** the savoury noodles on to a hot serving dish and
   sprinkle with the powdered prawns/shrimp and
   crushed peanuts.
8 **PLACE** the deep-fried bean curd squares in a bowl and pour
   boiling water over. Leave for 1 minute, then drain and slice.
9 **ARRANGE** the deep-fried bean curd slices around the edge
   of the serving dish with the remaining bean sprouts and top
   with the lacy omelette. Complete the garnish with chilli,
   coriander/cilantro leaves and spring onions/scallions and
   serve with lime or lemon wedges.

Soft-boiled Egg Noodles with Pork, Chicken or Prawns

Bah-Mee Haeng Moo, Gai or *Goong*

Golden egg noodles tossed with pork, chicken or prawns/shrimp in garlic-flavoured oil with bean sprouts and spring onions/scallions, moistened with fish sauce and garnished with dried powdered prawns/shrimp and plenty of coriander/cilantro. Dried noodles should be soaked for 10 minutes before being cooked. If using fresh noodles, shake lightly to untangle before use.

Serves 4 • Preparation time: 12 minutes • Cooking time: 15 minutes

225g/8oz fresh or dried egg noodles
175g/6oz boneless pork fillet or chicken breast, thinly sliced, or same weight shelled cooked prawns/shrimp
2 tbsp sunflower oil
1 garlic clove, crushed
225g/8oz/generous 2 cups bean sprouts
3 spring onions/scallions, finely shredded
1 tbsp fish sauce
1 tsp sugar
salt and freshly ground black pepper
1 tsp dried powdered prawns/shrimp (optional)
1 handful coriander/cilantro leaves, to garnish
1 recipe quantity sweet chilli dipping sauce (see page 27), to serve

1 **SOAK** the dried noodles, if using, in warm water for 10 minutes, then drain.

2 **BRING** 600ml/21fl oz/2½ cups water to the boil in a shallow frying pan, add the pork or chicken slices, return to the boil, turn the heat down, then simmer for 5–8 minutes, or until the meat slices are tender.

3 **LIFT** out the meat with a slotted spoon and reserve in a large bowl. Spoon out 6 tbsp of the cooking liquid and reserve. If using prawns/shrimp, use stock or water instead of the cooking liquid.

4 **BRING** plenty of salted water to the boil in a large saucepan, add the fresh or drained dried noodles and cook, stirring frequently, for 2–3 minutes. Drain, rinse with hot water and drain again. Add to the pork, chicken or prawns.

5 **HEAT** a wok, add the oil and, when hot, fry the garlic until golden. Do not let it turn brown or the oil may taste bitter.

6 **TOSS** in the meat or prawns and noodles from the bowl, then stir over a high heat briefly, adding sufficient reserved cooking liquid to moisten the noodles and meat or prawns. The mixture should be moist but not overly wet.

7 **ADD** the bean sprouts, spring onions/scallions, fish sauce, sugar and seasoning to taste.

8 **TURN** into hot serving bowls and sprinkle on the powdered dried prawns/shrimp, if using, and an abundance of coriander/cilantro leaves for a garnish.

9 **SERVE** with a bowl of sweet chilli dipping sauce to drizzle over each helping.

THE RECIPES

Thai cooking is fun, and real pleasure is to be had from both cooking and eating Thai dishes. Whether you prepare a tasty appetizer, a crisp stir-fry, a slow-cooked curry or a melt-in-the-mouth dessert, the flavours of Thailand will awaken your taste buds and transport you to the East. And you will be amazed at how easy many of these recipes are. With just a few ingredients and a quick cooking method, such as stir-frying, you can have a tasty oriental meal on the table in no time at all. Classic favourites such as Chicken Satay and Thai Fish Cakes intermingle here with less familiar dishes, such as Pumpkin and Coconut Cream Soup, Jungle Curry, Steamed Stuffed Crabs and Mango Sorbet – all of which will delight the palate.

When serving Thai food, it is usual to have a large bowl of fluffy rice in the centre of the table. Each diner then takes a portion of rice and a little helping from each of the dishes in turn. Soups are sipped throughout the meal, rather than being served first. Simple desserts, which are often fruit based, round off the meal. Such a combination of tastes and textures makes Thai food unbeatable.

Prawn Toasts

Kanom Pang Nah-Goong

A stunning blend of pork fat and prawns/shrimp with traditional Thai flavourings and a hint of crunchy water chestnut, spread on bread triangles, deep-fried to a golden crunchiness and served with a sweet and sour cucumber relish.

Makes 24 • Preparation time: 30 minutes • Cooking time: 12–15 minutes

6 slices bread, 2–3 days old
2 tsp sesame seeds
sunflower oil, for deep-frying
1 recipe quantity Thai relish (see page 28)

FOR THE TOPPING
55g/2oz pork fat (small cubes from the butcher)
225g/8oz peeled cooked prawns/shrimp
6 water chestnuts
2 coriander/cilantro stems
1 garlic clove, crushed
1 tbsp fish sauce
1 tsp sugar
1 tbsp cornflour/cornstarch
1 egg white, lightly beaten
salt and freshly ground black pepper

1 **BLEND** the cubes of pork fat in a food processor for a few seconds, then add the prawns/shrimp and other topping ingredients and blend to a smooth paste.

2 **SPREAD** the mixture onto the bread slices. Trim the crusts and cut each slice into 4 triangles or squares. Scatter with the sesame seeds, pressing them in lightly.

3 **PLACE** on a tray lined with baking parchment, adding more parchment between the layers to prevent the toasts sticking to each other. If not being cooked immediately, cover loosely with cling film/plastic wrap and refrigerate until required. (If the prawns were frozen, use the mixture soon after preparation.)

4 **HEAT** the oil in a wok or deep saucepan to 190°C/375°F and fry several pieces at a time, paste side down, until crisp and golden, turning once. Drain on paper towels and serve with a little relish spooned on top.

Steamed Dumplings
Kanom Jeeb

Tiny, light and luscious dumplings packed with fresh pork or prawns/shrimp or crunchy vegetables, expertly flavoured with coriander/cilantro, garlic, soy sauce and zingy fresh chilli, served with a traditional Thai soy dipping sauce.

Makes 30 • Preparation time: 30 minutes • Cooking time: 20–24 minutes

225g/8oz finely minced/ground pork
55g/2oz peeled raw prawns/shrimp or
    4–6 water chestnuts or 1 small carrot, finely
    grated
1 garlic clove, crushed
1 coriander/cilantro stem
1 tbsp soy sauce
1 red or green chilli, deseeded and
    finely chopped
salt and freshly ground black pepper
1 egg, beaten
30 wonton wrappers (7.5cm/3in square),
    thawed if frozen
1 recipe quantity dark soy dipping sauce (see
    page 27)

1 **PLACE** the pork in a food processor with the prawns/shrimp, water chestnuts or carrot, garlic, coriander/cilantro stalk and leaves, soy sauce, chilli and seasoning. Blend to a smooth paste with half the beaten egg.

2 **PLACE** 2 wrappers at a time on a clean work surface, covering the other wrappers with a clean damp cloth. Place a tiny spoonful of the mixture on each wrapper.

3 **BRUSH** lightly around the edge of the wrapper with the remaining beaten egg, then pull up the edges to form a purse shape. Press to seal. If preparing ahead, place the dumplings in a single layer on a tray, cover loosely with cling film/plastic wrap and chill, or freeze, until needed.

4 **CUT** a sheet of non-stick baking parchment into strips and place the dumplings on these in a steamer. Cook the dumplings in two batches over boiling water for 10–12 minutes if cooking from fresh (14–16 minutes if cooking from frozen).

5 **SERVE** hot with the soy dipping sauce.

Thai Spring Rolls
Pow-Pia Tawd

Crisp, golden spring/egg rolls encasing a sumptuous mixture of Chinese mushrooms, bean sprouts, chicken or pork and noodles, served with a plum sauce.

Makes 12 • Preparation time: 25 minutes, plus 20–30 minutes soaking time • Cooking time: 8–10 minutes

24 spring/egg roll wrappers (12.5cm/
    5in square), thawed if frozen
½ egg, beaten
cornflour/cornstarch (optional)
sunflower oil, for deep-frying
1 recipe quantity preserved plum dipping
    sauce (see page 27)

FOR THE FILLING
4 Chinese mushrooms
25g/1oz bean thread noodles
3 tbsp sunflower oil
175g/6oz finely minced/ground chicken breast
    or pork
100g/3½oz/1 cup bean sprouts
1 carrot, finely grated
1 garlic clove, crushed
2 coriander/cilantro stems, stalks and leaves
    chopped
salt and freshly ground black pepper

1 **SOAK** the mushrooms in warm water for 20–30 minutes, then drain, discard the stalks and slice the mushroom caps very finely. Meanwhile, soak the noodles in warm water for 10 minutes until soft, then drain and cut into small pieces with scissors.

2 **HEAT** a wok, add the 3 tbsp of oil, then the chicken or pork and stir-fry for 2–3 minutes. Add the remaining filling ingredients and toss well over a moderate heat for 2–3 minutes. Turn onto a plate and allow to cool.

3 **PLACE** 2 spring roll wrappers at a time on a clean work surface, covering the others with a damp cloth. Place a spoonful of filling on each wrapper and roll up one turn.

4 **TURN** the sides to the middle and continue rolling into a neat shape, brushing a little beaten egg onto the tip to seal each spring roll.

5 **PLACE** in a single layer on a clean plate dusted lightly with a little cornflour/cornstarch or on a sheet of non-stick baking parchment.

6 **HEAT** the oil for deep-frying to 190°C/375°F. Deep-fry several spring rolls at a time until golden. This will take 2 minutes. Drain on plenty of paper towels. Serve hot with the preserved plum dipping sauce.

Prawn Satay

Goong Satay

Makes 16 • Preparation time: 10 minutes, plus 30 minutes marinating time • Cooking time: 3–4 minutes

2 tsp sugar
6 coriander/cilantro stems, stalks only
1 garlic clove
1cm/½in piece fresh root ginger, peeled and sliced
½ green chilli, deseeded and finely shredded
3 tbsp sunflower oil
16 large raw prawns/shrimp, heads removed, peeled but tails left on
1 recipe quantity peanut sauce (see page 28), to serve
lettuce leaves and chunks of cucumber, to serve

1 **SOAK** 16 bamboo or wooden skewers in water to cover.

2 **PLACE** the sugar, coriander/cilantro stalks, garlic, ginger and chilli in a mortar with the oil and use a pestle to pound to a fragrant paste. Pour the paste over the prawns/shrimp, mix thoroughly and leave to marinate for 30 minutes while you make the peanut sauce.

3 **THREAD** the prawns onto the soaked skewers. Place under a hot grill/broiler until the prawns are pink and cooked, turning as necessary. Allow about 3–4 minutes only.

4 **SERVE** with the peanut sauce and chunks of cucumber on a lettuce-lined serving dish.

VARIATION Chicken, Pork and Beef Satay Gai, Moo and Neau Satay

Chill 225g/8oz each of chicken breast, lean pork and beef fillet in the freezer for 30 minutes before cutting into neat, even-sized pieces, keeping the meats separate. Prepare the marinade by stirring 250ml/9fl oz/1 cup coconut milk, 1 tsp ground turmeric, 1 tsp hot or mild curry powder to taste and a pinch of salt together. Pour this over the chicken and pork pieces. For the beef satay, sprinkle the meat with ground cumin before pouring the marinade over it. Leave all the meats to marinate for at least 1 hour. Thread the meats separately onto soaked wooden skewers just before cooking. Cook under a hot grill/broiler or over a barbecue, brushing with some of the marinade. Turn frequently until cooked through. Serve on a large plate with peanut sauce (see page 28) and cucumber salad (see page 146) or pieces of onion and cucumber.

Thai Fish Cakes

Tawd Mun Pla

Delicate little fish cakes, crisp and golden on the outside, moist and tasty on the inside, flavoured with red curry paste, green beans, lime leaves and fish sauce.

Makes 24 • Preparation time: 20–25 minutes • Cooking time: 10–12 minutes

550g/1¼lb cod or haddock fillet
2 tsp red curry paste (see page 24)
1 tbsp fish sauce
2 tbsp cornflour/cornstarch
55g/2oz long or green beans, finely sliced
3 lime leaves, very finely shredded
½ egg, beaten
salt and freshly ground black pepper
sunflower oil, to cover bottom of pan
8 lemon grass stems, top parts only

FOR THE CRUNCHY SWEET CHILLI SAUCE
4 tbsp sweet chilli dipping sauce
  (see page 27)
½ small carrot, finely diced
2.5cm/1in piece cucumber, finely diced
2 coriander/cilantro stems, leaves
  roughly torn
2 tbsp roasted peanuts, lightly crushed

1 **SKIN** and bone the fish, then cut into pieces and process briefly in a food processor. Add the curry paste, fish sauce, cornflour,/cornstarch beans and lime leaves, then process again briefly. Finally, add just sufficient beaten egg to bind the mixture. Season well.

2 **FORM** into even-size fish cakes with a hole in the centre. Chill, if time allows, or freeze for future use if required.

3 **PUT** the dipping sauce in a serving bowl. Add the carrot and cucumber and add a few torn coriander/cilantro leaves. Cover and chill. Stir in the lightly crushed peanuts and remaining coriander leaves just before serving.

4 **SHALLOW-FRY** the fish cakes in hot oil for 2–3 minutes on each side (3–4 minutes if frozen), depending on the size.

5 **THREAD** 3 fish cakes onto each lemon grass stem and serve with the sauce, to be spooned onto each fish cake in turn.

Prawns in Blankets

Kung Hom Pa

This is a variation on the spring/egg roll. You need large fresh prawns/shrimp with tails intact so that they project out of one end of the roll. The prawns are cut in half to hasten the cooking, then combined with a spicy, crunchy pork stuffing.

Makes 16 • Preparation time: 25 minutes • Cooking time: 6–10 minutes

16 large raw prawns/shrimp, heads removed, shelled but tails left on
16 spring/egg roll wrappers (12.5cm/ 5in square), thawed if frozen
½ egg, beaten
sunflower oil, for deep-frying
1 recipe quantity sweet chilli dipping sauce (see page 27)

FOR THE STUFFING
55g/2oz minced/ground pork
6 water chestnuts
1 spring onion/scallion, chopped
1cm/½in piece fresh root ginger, peeled and sliced
1 tsp fish sauce
freshly ground black pepper

1 **CUT** each prawn/shrimp in half along the back, then open out, removing the vein if necessary.

2 **PREPARE** the stuffing. Mix the pork, water chestnuts, spring onion/ scallion, ginger and fish sauce in a food processor with pepper to make a fine paste.

3 **SPREAD** out 4 spring roll wrappers on a clean work surface, covering the others with a clean damp cloth, and place a small spoonful of stuffing on each wrapper near the lower edge. Lay a prawn on top of the stuffing with the tail exposed.

4 **FOLD** each wrapper over toward the tail, then brush the edges with beaten egg and roll up, with the prawn tail exposed. Make up the remainder of the rolls in the same way and place in a single layer on a tray lined with baking parchment.

5 **HEAT** the oil for deep-frying in a wok or deep saucepan to 190°C/375°F, and fry several of the wrapped prawns at a time for 2–3 minutes until golden. Drain on crumpled paper towels.

6 **SERVE** with a bowl of sweet chilli dipping sauce alongside.

Nam Prik Sauce with Crudités

Nam Prik Pak Jeem

In Thailand this is the universal sauce. It is used as a dip and is usually served with colourful fresh vegetable "dippers" and some puffy prawn crackers/shrimp chips. The sauce can also be served simply stirred into a bowl of rice as a light meal.

Serves 4–5 • Preparation time: 15 minutes, plus 15 minutes soaking time

55g/2oz dried prawns/shrimp
1cm/½in cube prepared kapi (see page 15)
2–3 garlic cloves, crushed
1–3 red or green chillies, deseeded and chopped
55g/2oz shelled cooked prawns/shrimp
1 large coriander/cilantro stem
12 tiny pea aubergines/eggplants
2 tbsp fish sauce
3–4 tbsp lemon juice
1 tbsp dark brown sugar
selection of vegetable crudités, such as cucumber, carrot, celery, tomato, plus prawn crackers/shrimp chips and pork crackling (see page 18)

1 **SOAK** the dried prawns/shrimp in water for 15 minutes, then drain. Place them with the prepared kapi, garlic and chillies (the number depending on how hot you like your food) in a food processor and blend.

2 **ADD** the cooked prawns/shrimp and most of the coriander/cilantro stalks and leaves, reserving some of the leaves for a garnish. Add the aubergines/eggplants and process again. Now add the seasonings of fish sauce, lemon juice and sugar to taste. Add a little water if you feel that the sauce is too thick, but this should not be necessary.

3 **ARRANGE** the selected vegetables, the prawn crackers/shrimp chips and pork crackling attractively on a serving dish and place the sauce in a bowl in the centre for dipping. This can be made up in advance, covered in cling film/plastic wrap and chilled until required.

4 **GARNISH** the sauce with the reserved coriander leaves just before serving. (Any leftover sauce can be stored in a glass screw-top jar with cling film under the lid for a week.)

Prawn Crackers

Khow Grieb Goong

Light-as-air prawn crackers/shrimp chips, ready to dip into sweet chilli sauce (*nam prik waan*), tangy yet sweet preserved plum sauce (*nam bouy*) and dark soy sauce (*si-ew waan*), make a delicious pre-dinner nibble with drinks.

Serves 4 • Preparation time: 2 minutes • Cooking time: 4–5 minutes

sunflower oil, for deep-frying
55–85g/2–3oz uncooked prawn crackers/
   shrimp chips
selection of dipping sauces (see page 27)

1 **HEAT** the oil in a wok or deep saucepan to 190°C/375°F. Line a tray with a double layer of crumpled paper towels.

2 **DEEP-FRY** only 8–10 prawn crackers/shrimp chips at a time, as they swell up considerably in size. Keep them moving as they cook, which will take only 10–20 seconds. Take care not to cook in oil that is too hot. They should remain white or pale pink after cooking.

3 **LIFT** out with a slotted spoon and drain on paper towels. Serve with any or all of the dipping sauces on page 27. Any leftovers keep well in an airtight plastic container.

Money Bags
Thung Thong

Makes 20 • Preparation time: 30 minutes, plus 20–30 minutes soaking time • Cooking time: 9–12 minutes

40 spring/egg roll wrappers (12.5cm/
    5in square), thawed if frozen
½ egg, beaten
sunflower oil, for deep-frying
1 recipe quantity sweet chilli dipping sauce
    (see page 27)

FOR THE FILLING
3 Chinese mushrooms
25g/1oz bean thread noodles
1 garlic clove
8 black peppercorns
2 coriander/cilantro stems
200g/7oz minced/ground pork
100g/3½oz shelled cooked prawns/shrimp
2 tbsp sunflower oil, for frying
1 tsp sugar
1 tbsp fish sauce
5 spring onions/scallions with long green tops,
    green parts only

1 **SOAK** the Chinese mushrooms in warm water for 20–30 minutes, then drain. Remove the stalks and slice the caps finely. Meanwhile, soak the bean thread noodles in warm water for 10 minutes until soft, then drain.

2 **POUND** the garlic, peppercorns and coriander/cilantro stalks and root (if available) together, reserving the coriander leaves for a garnish.

3 **MIX** the minced/ground pork with the prawns/shrimp in a food processor. Turn into a bowl. With scissors, snip the bean thread noodles into short lengths.

4 **HEAT** the oil and fry the coriander mixture until it gives off a fragrant aroma. Add the pork, prawns, noodles and mushrooms. Cook for 3–4 minutes until the pork is cooked, stirring and tossing so that the mixture is well broken up. Add the sugar and fish sauce. Remove from the heat and allow to cool.

5 **PLUNGE** the long green tops of the spring onions/scallions into boiling water, then put directly into cold water. Drain well and set aside.

6 **USE** 2 wrappers for each money bag. Place one square in front of you and one with the points over the straight sides. Place a small spoonful of filling in the centre of each stack, brush the edge with egg to seal, then form into a sack shape. Tie attractively with the drained spring onion tops and secure with a cocktail stick/toothpick if necessary.

7 **HEAT** the oil for deep-frying in a wok or deep saucepan to 190°C/375°F, then deep-fry the money bags in batches for 3 minutes or until crispy and golden brown. Lift out and drain on paper towels.

8 **PLACE** on a serving dish and serve with the sweet chilli dipping sauce.

Corn Cakes
Tawd Mun Kow Pod

Tender minced/ground pork, juicy corn, fragrant lime leaves and a dash of red curry paste, blended together to make mouth-watering, crisp-fried morsels topped with the wonderful contrasting flavours of a sweet spicy dipping sauce or Thai relish.

Makes 24 • Preparation time: 30 minutes • Cooking time: 6–8 minutes

1 can sweetcorn (320g/11oz/1¼ cups), drained
280g/10oz finely minced/ground pork
2 tsp red curry paste (see page 24)
1 tbsp soy sauce
3 tbsp cornflour/cornstarch
4 lime leaves, finely shredded
1 coriander/cilantro stem
2 tsp sugar
½ egg, beaten
sunflower oil, for frying
lettuce leaves, to serve
1 recipe quantity sweet chilli dipping sauce or Thai relish (see pages 27 or 28)

1 **PLACE** the sweetcorn in a bowl with the pork, curry paste, soy sauce, cornflour/cornstarch and shredded lime leaves. Chop the coriander/cilantro stalk (reserving the leaves for a garnish) and add to the mixture.

2 **BLEND** together well by hand, then add the sugar and slowly add just sufficient beaten egg to bind.

3 **FORM** into small cakes, using the flat blade of a knife lightly brushed with oil, and place on a well-floured baking tray.

4 **SHALLOW-FRY** for about 3–5 minutes in hot oil on both sides until brown and cooked through. Drain on paper towels.

5 **GARNISH** with the coriander leaves and serve with lettuce. Spoon a little sauce or relish on to each corn cake before eating.

Lettuce Parcels

Mieng Kam or *Khana Haw*

A dish of fresh lettuce, wafer-thin lemon, shredded chilli and ginger, crunchy salted peanuts
and plump prawns/shrimp. Allow your guests to make up their own parcels using as much
or as little of the spices as their taste buds will allow.

Serves 4 • Preparation time: 25 minutes

8 lettuce leaves from a round, soft lettuce
4 paper-thin slices of lemon, quartered
1 red and 1 green chilli, shredded
2.5cm/1in piece fresh root ginger, shredded
1 handful salted peanuts
32 shelled cooked prawns/shrimp or
  16 shelled cooked tiger prawns/shrimp (can
  be cut in half)
8 small lemon wedges

1 **PLACE** the lettuce leaves, which must be completely dry, in one bowl and divide the remaining ingredients into four small piles or ramekin dishes on a central serving dish.

2 **INVITE** each diner to place a lettuce leaf on their plate, place half the filling ingredients on top and finish with a squeeze of lemon. The leaf should then be rolled up into a neat parcel and eaten at once, before the second lettuce parcel is made with the remaining ingredients.

Coconut Crisps
Mapraow Krua

This recipe for coconut crisps may sound as if a lot of effort is required,
but the enthusiasm of your guests will make it all worthwhile.

**Makes 425g/15oz • Preparation time:
25 minutes • Cooking time: 30 minutes**

1 large fresh coconut
2 tbsp sea salt

1 **PREHEAT** the oven to 170°C/325°F/Gas 3.

2 **OPEN** the coconut (see page 12) and use a knife to ease the two halves
apart. Crack into smaller pieces if necessary.

3 **SLIDE** the blade of a palette knife/metal spatula between the white flesh
and brown husk of the coconut to ease away the hard outer casing. If you
prefer to remove the remaining brown skin, do so using a potato peeler,
but this is not essential.

4 **FIT** the fine-slicing blade attachment to your food processor, then feed
the peeled pieces of coconut down the feed tube. (If not all the coconut
slices are required now, place the remainder on an open tray and freeze
for future use.)

5 **PLACE** the thin coconut slices on a baking sheet, sprinkle with salt and
bake in the preheated oven for 30 minutes. Turn twice to ensure even
cooking. Cool before serving.

Beef Soup with Noodles
Guay Tiew Nam-Neau

Rice noodles, tender beef strips and crunchy bean sprouts gently submerged
in a rich, garlicky beef stock with the warm fragrances of cinnamon and galangal.

**Serves 4 • Preparation time: 20 minutes
• Cooking time: 35 minutes**

1 litre/35fl oz/4¼ cups beef stock or
 diluted consommé
3 coriander/cilantro stems
½ bunch spring onions/scallions,
 finely chopped
1cm/½in piece galangal, bruised
1 cinnamon stick
115g/4oz flat dried rice noodles
 or 225g/8oz flat fresh rice noodles
2 tbsp sunflower oil
115g/4oz beef fillet/filet mignon, cut into
 sticks
1 garlic clove, crushed
1–2 tbsp fish sauce
1 tbsp dark soy sauce
juice of ½ lemon or lime
freshly ground black pepper
55g/2oz/¼ cup bean sprouts
1 small red or green chilli, finely sliced

1 **POUR** the stock into a saucepan. Crush the coriander/cilantro stalks (reserving the leaves for a garnish) and add along with half the spring onions/scallions, the galangal and cinnamon stick. Bring to the boil, then turn the heat down and simmer for 20 minutes. Remove the galangal and cinnamon stick.

2 **SOAK** the flat dried rice noodles, if using, in warm water for 15 minutes while the stock is simmering, then drain.

3 **HEAT** the oil in a frying pan and fry the beef strips and garlic until the beef changes colour. Add to the stock with the fish sauce to taste, the soy sauce, lemon or lime juice and pepper to taste. Bring to the boil and simmer for 5 minutes. Taste again and adjust the seasoning if necessary.

4 **PLACE** the drained dried rice noodles, if using, in a large saucepan of boiling water and cook for 2 minutes. Drain well, rinse through with boiling water in a colander. If using fresh rice noodles, cut into fine strips and plunge into boiling water for 1 minute. Drain, rinse and drain again.

5 **DIVIDE** the noodles and bean sprouts between four soup bowls. Spoon over the hot soup and garnish with the remaining spring onions, coriander leaves and shredded chillies.

Clear Soup with Stuffed Mushrooms

Gaeng Jued Hed

Chinese mushrooms stuffed with pork, garlic, coriander/cilantro, spring onions/scallions
and crunchy water chestnuts, moistened with soy sauce then steamed and served in a
full-bodied chicken stock laced with fish sauce.

**Serves 4 • Preparation time: 12–15 minutes,
plus 20–30 minutes soaking time
• Cooking time: 15 minutes**

8 small Chinese mushrooms or shiitake or
    button mushrooms
1 litre/35fl oz/4¼ cups chicken stock (see
    page 23)
1–2 tbsp fish sauce
1 handful young spinach leaves

FOR THE STUFFING
55g/2oz finely minced/ground pork with
    some pork fat
½ garlic clove, crushed
1 coriander/cilantro stem
½–1 tsp soy sauce
1 spring onion/scallion, chopped
3 water chestnuts
salt and freshly ground black pepper

1 **SOAK** the mushrooms in 150ml/5fl oz/⅔ cup warm water for
20–30 minutes. Pour the soaking water into a saucepan with the stock.
(If using fresh mushrooms, add extra vegetable stock or water.)

2 **DISCARD** the stalks from the Chinese mushrooms and leave the
caps whole. Remove the stalks from the button mushrooms, if using.

3 **PLACE** the pork in a food processor with the garlic and coriander/
cilantro stalks (reserve the leaves for a garnish). Add the soy sauce, spring
onion/scallion, water chestnuts and seasoning, then process to a paste.

4 **DIVIDE** the mixture between the mushrooms. Place on strips of
non-stick baking parchment in a bamboo or metal steamer over boiling
water, cover and steam for 15 minutes.

5 **BRING** the stock to the boil in the meantime. Add the fish sauce and
season to taste.

6 **PLACE** the steamed mushrooms in soup bowls with the coriander leaves
and tiny pieces of torn spinach and pour over the boiling stock.

Clear Soup with Wontons

Giew Nam

A steaming bowl of tiny dumplings filled with a sumptuous mixture of pork or prawns/shrimp, garlic, coriander/cilantro and fish sauce, topped with crunchy bean sprouts or shredded Chinese leaves, floating in a rich fish or chicken stock.

Serves 6 • Preparation time: 25–35 minutes • Cooking time: 6 minutes

115g/4oz lean minced/ground pork or shelled cooked prawns/shrimp
½ garlic clove, crushed
2 coriander/cilantro stems
2 tsp soy or fish sauce
freshly ground black pepper
½ egg, beaten
18 wonton wrappers (7.5cm/3in square), thawed if frozen
1.25 litres/40fl oz/5 cups chicken or fish stock (see page 23)
115g/4oz/generous 1 cup bean sprouts or finely shredded Chinese leaves
1 green chilli, deseeded and finely chopped, to garnish

1 **BLEND** the pork or prawns/shrimp with the garlic and coriander/cilantro stalks (reserving the leaves for garnish) in a food processor. When smooth, add the soy or fish sauce, pepper and just enough egg to bind, reserving the remainder for sealing the wontons.

2 **PLACE** several wonton wrappers at a time on a clean work surface (covering the rest with a clean damp cloth) and place a tiny spoonful of the mixture on each one. Brush the edges with a little of the beaten egg.

3 **FOLD** into purse shapes, sealing the tops well. Alternatively, roll up into mini spring/egg roll shapes, damping the last edges to seal. Whichever shape you choose, the wontons should be bite-size.

4 **LEAVE** covered until required. If they are to be kept for a while, place them on baking parchment so that they will not stick to the surface of the plate or box.

5 **BRING** a saucepan of water to the boil and cook the wontons in this in two batches for 3 minutes. Meanwhile, bring the stock to the boil.

6 **LIFT** the wontons out of the water with a slotted spoon and divide among six soup bowls. Top with the bean sprouts or shredded Chinese leaves and pour over the boiling soup. Serve garnished with chopped chilli and the reserved coriander leaves.

Chicken Soup with Coconut
Tom Kha Gai

This fragrant, creamy-textured soup, with its thin slivers of tender chicken, has a deceptive bite from the fresh red chillies nestling in its midst. Stop to smell the fabulous blend of aromas before you take the first spoonful.

Serves 4 • Preparation time: 8–10 minutes • Cooking time: 12–15 minutes

1 can coconut milk (400ml/14fl oz/1²/₃ cups)
570ml/20fl oz/scant 2½ cups chicken stock (see page 23)
2cm/¾in piece galangal, peeled and finely sliced
2 red chillies, deseeded and sliced
1 lemon grass stem, lower 6cm/2½in sliced
3 lime leaves, torn into pieces
4 tbsp fish sauce
2 tbsp lemon juice
1 tsp sugar
1 chicken breast (about 175g/6oz), cut into slivers
coriander/cilantro leaves, to garnish

1 **POUR** the coconut milk into a saucepan, stirring over a gentle heat to make sure that the milk is smooth. Stir in one direction only to prevent the milk curdling.

2 **HEAT** the prepared stock in a much larger saucepan with 300ml/10½fl oz/1¼ cups water, galangal, chillies, lemon grass and torn lime leaves.

3 **STIR** in the warmed coconut milk, then add the fish sauce, lemon juice and sugar. Allow to come to the boil, then reduce the heat and simmer for 5 minutes. Taste and adjust the seasoning.

4 **BRING** back to the boil, drop in the chicken slivers a few at a time so that they remain separate. Cook for 3–4 minutes until the chicken pieces are cooked.

5 **SERVE** garnished with coriander/cilantro leaves.

Chiang Mai Curried Noodle Soup with Chicken Khao

Soi Gai

Serves 4 • Preparation time: 35 minutes • Cooking time: 30 minutes

1 chicken (1.25kg/2lb 12oz), skinned
1½ cans coconut milk (600ml/29fl oz/3½ cups)
1–2 tbsp red curry paste (see page 24)
1 tsp ground turmeric
825ml/1½ pints/generous 3 cups chicken stock (see page 23)
2–3 tbsp fish sauce
2 tbsp soy sauce
juice of 1 lime
1 handful coriander/cilantro leaves, roughly chopped
300–400g/10½–14oz fresh or dried egg noodles (if using dried, soak for 10 minutes)

FOR THE GARNISHES
sunflower oil, for deep-frying
55g/2oz dried egg noodles
1–2 red chillies, deseeded and finely sliced
4 shallots, finely sliced
4 spring onions/scallions, sliced
1 can fermented mustard greens (140g/5oz), finely sliced

1 **CUT** the chicken meat into bite-size pieces. (The legs can be kept in the refrigerator for use in another recipe if liked.)

2 **POUR** the contents of one can of coconut milk into a wok or large saucepan. Stir over a medium heat until the milk begins to curdle, then add the curry paste and turmeric. Stir to make a rich sauce, then reduce the heat and cook for 3 minutes.

3 **ADD** the chicken and turn in the spicy mixture until well coated. Pour in the remaining coconut milk, stock, fish sauce to taste and soy sauce, then cook over a medium heat for 8 minutes until the chicken is tender. Add the lime juice and scatter with most of the coriander/cilantro leaves.

4 **PREPARE** the garnishes by deep-frying the noodles until crisp. Drain on paper towels, then lightly crush to add texture and crunch to the soup. Place with the other garnishes in small ramekin dishes.

5 **PLUNGE** the fresh noodles into boiling water, then drain. If using dried noodles, place them in boiling salted water. Return to the boil and cook for 5 minutes or according to the package directions. Drain, rinse with boiling water and drain again.

6 **PLACE** the noodles in warmed bowls and pour on the soup. Top with the remaining coriander leaves and some crushed fried noodles.

7 **HAND** around the other garnishes at the table.

Hot and Sour Prawn Soup

Tom Yum Goong

Prawns/shrimp and squid are gently simmered in homemade stock, flavoured with the delicate fragrance of lemon grass, galangal and lime leaves and the essential fish sauce, before being garnished with sliced red chilli and fresh coriander/cilantro.

Serves 4 • Preparation time: 15 minutes
• Cooking time: 18–20 minutes

750ml/26fl oz/3¼ cups fish or chicken stock
  (see page 23)
1 lemon grass stem
4 red bird's eye chillies, deseeded and finely
  sliced
2.5cm/1in piece galangal, peeled and finely
  sliced
3 lime leaves, torn into pieces
2–3 ready-cleaned squid
12 shelled cooked tiger prawns/shrimp
  or 250g/9oz small shelled prawns/shrimp
1 can straw mushrooms (220g/7¾oz), drained
  or 4 button mushrooms, sliced
juice of 1 large lemon
1 tsp sugar
2–3 tbsp fish sauce
1 red chilli, deseeded and finely sliced,
  to garnish
coriander/cilantro leaves, to garnish

1 **PLACE** the stock in a large saucepan with 300ml/10½fl oz/1¼ cups water. Heat gently.

2 **TRIM** the root from the lemon grass and slice the bottom 5cm/2in section into fine slices. Bruise the remaining stalk and add all this to the stock with the chillies, galangal and 2 of the torn lime leaves.

3 **BRING** to the boil, reduce the heat and simmer gently for 10 minutes to blend all the flavours.

4 **PREPARE** the squid and cut into strips or rings (see page 19).

5 **REMOVE** the bruised lemon grass, add the prawns/shrimp, squid and the mushrooms, then add the lemon juice, sugar and fish sauce a little at a time, testing as you do, until you have the right balance of flavours.

6 **SERVE** in bowls with slices of red chilli, the remaining torn lime leaf and a few coriander/cilantro leaves floating on top.

Mixed Seafood and Coconut Soup
Tom Kha Talay

Cod, squid and prawns/shrimp cooked in a spiced stock blended with coconut milk
and flavoured with turmeric – a seafood soup to remember.

**Serves 4 • Preparation time: 20 minutes
• Cooking time: 10 minutes**

175g/6oz cod, skinned and cut into cubes
175g/6oz ready-cleaned squid
12 shelled cooked tiger prawns/shrimp
1 can coconut milk (400ml/14fl oz/1²/₃ cups)
1 tsp ground turmeric
750ml/26fl oz/3¼ cups fish stock (see page 23)
2 lemon grass stems, lower 6cm/2½in
    finely sliced
2cm/¾in piece galangal, peeled and finely
    sliced
3 lime leaves, torn
2 red or green chillies, deseeded and
    finely sliced
4 tbsp fish sauce
3 tbsp lime or lemon juice
1–2 dried chillies, deseeded and broken
    into pieces
1 small handful coriander/cilantro leaves

1 **ASSEMBLE** the fresh fish pieces and seafood, which should total around 500g/1lb 2oz. Prepare the squid and cut into rings or strips (see page 19). Arrange on a plate, cover and chill.

2 **POUR** one-third of the can of coconut milk into a saucepan. Heat gently and, when bubbling, add the turmeric and cook for 1 minute, stirring all the time, to bring out the flavour. Stir in the remaining coconut milk and mix thoroughly until all the coconut is incorporated and smooth. Remove from the heat.

3 **HEAT** the stock and 300ml/10½fl oz/1¼ cups water in a separate saucepan. Add the lemon
grass, galangal, lime leaves and fresh chillies. Bring to the boil and simmer for 5 minutes to bring out the flavour.

4 **ADD** the coconut milk and turmeric mixture, the fish sauce and lime or lemon juice. Taste for seasoning.

5 **BRING** the soup to the boil, add the fish pieces and seafood, return to the boil, then turn the heat down and simmer for 3–4 minutes only.

6 **SERVE** at once, garnished with the dried chilli pieces and coriander/cilantro leaves.

Pumpkin and Coconut Cream Soup
Gaeng Liang Fak Tong

An unusual soup that gets its creamy texture from blending spices and prawns/shrimp into a liquid paste. If you wish, add some fresh prawns just before serving.

Serves 4 • Preparation time: 12 minutes, plus 15 minutes soaking time • Cooking time: 30 minutes

55g/2oz dried prawns/shrimp
1 onion, quartered
2cm/¾in piece fresh root ginger, peeled
2 red or green chillies, deseeded
1 lemon grass stem, lower 6cm/2½in cut in three and top of stem bruised
350ml/12fl oz/1⅓ cups chicken or fish stock (see page 23) or water
1 can coconut milk (400ml/14fl oz/1²/₃ cups)
2 tbsp fish sauce
1 tsp sugar
freshly ground black pepper
400g/14oz pumpkin, peeled, deseeded and diced
1 small handful basil leaves
115g/4oz shelled cooked prawns/shrimp (optional)

1 **SOAK** the dried prawns/shrimp in 150ml/5fl oz/⅔ cup warm water for 15 minutes.

2 **PROCESS** the onion, ginger, chillies and lower part of the lemon grass with the soaked prawns and their liquid in a food processor until well blended.

3 **POUR** the stock or water into a large saucepan and add the coconut milk. Combine well.

4 **HEAT** until nearly boiling, then pour in the spice mixture and stir over a gentle heat until the soup is well blended. Add the fish sauce to taste, the sugar and black pepper.

5 **RETURN** to the boil, then turn the heat down and simmer the soup for 5 minutes. Add the pumpkin dice, lemon grass stem and some basil leaves (reserve a few to garnish). Cook for a further 20 minutes, stirring from time to time and checking with a skewer to see whether the pumpkin is tender. Remove the lemon grass stem. Add the peeled prawns/shrimp, if using.

6 **SERVE** hot in bowls with the remaining basil leaves, torn.

Hot and Sour Vegetable Soup

Tom Yum Pak

A stunningly colourful clear soup full of stir-fried baby corn, mushrooms, carrots and spinach, laced with lemon or lime, lemon grass and galangal and spiked with chillies.

Serves 4 • Preparation time: 5–8 minutes • Cooking time: 15 minutes

1 litre/35fl oz/4¼ cups vegetable or chicken stock (see page 23)
2 lemon grass stems, lower 5cm/2in sliced
1cm/½in piece galangal, scraped and finely sliced
2 chillies, deseeded and sliced
2 coriander/cilantro stems
3 lime leaves, torn into pieces
1–2 tbsp fish sauce
juice of 1–2 limes or 1 large lemon
salt and freshly ground black pepper
1 tsp sugar
4 baby sweetcorn, finely sliced
8 button mushrooms, finely sliced
1 carrot, finely diced
2 tbsp sunflower oil
1 handful spinach, shredded

1 **POUR** the stock and into a large saucepan with 300ml/10½fl oz/1¼ cups water, add the lemon grass, galangal and 1 of the chillies, the chopped coriander/cilantro stalks (reserve the leaves for garnish) and the lime leaves.

2 **BRING** to the boil, then reduce the heat and simmer for 10 minutes. Add the fish sauce and sufficient lime or lemon juice to give a tart flavour. Taste as you add the lime or lemon juice to get the right balance of flavour. Adjust the seasoning and add a little sugar, if liked.

3 **ASSEMBLE** the prepared vegetables (apart from the spinach) in a large bowl. Heat the oil in a saucepan, add the vegetables and toss everything together for 1 minute.

4 **ADD** to the boiling soup, adding the spinach at the last moment in order to retain its rich colour.

5 **GARNISH** the soup with the reserved coriander leaves and the remaining chilli, if liked.

Thai Beef Salad

Yum Neau

Beef fillet/filet mignon, perfectly cooked to a delicate pink, then cut into wafer-thin slices, tossed with matchsticks of carrot and cucumber, red onion, spring onions/scallions and a tangy yet fiery dressing, garnished with mint and coriander/cilantro.

Serves 4 • Preparation time: 15–20 minutes • Cooking time: 4–6 minutes

225g/8oz beef fillet/filet mignon
salt and freshly ground black pepper
3 tbsp fish sauce
juice of 1 large lime or lemon
1 tbsp sugar
1 red chilli, deseeded and finely sliced
4 shallots or 1 small red onion, finely sliced
2 garlic cloves, crushed
2 lemon grass stems, lower 5cm/2in finely sliced
1/3 cucumber, cut into matchsticks or coarsely grated
2 carrots, cut into matchsticks or coarsely grated
2–3 spring onions/scallions, finely shredded
1 small handful each coriander/cilantro and mint leaves

1 **SEASON** the beef, then place it under a hot grill/broiler. Cook to medium-rare (about 4–6 minutes, depending on thickness), turning twice during cooking. Allow to rest for 10 minutes before slicing thinly.

2 **BLEND** the fish sauce with the lime or lemon juice, sugar, chilli and half the shallots or onion to make the dressing.

3 **TOSS** the beef slices with the garlic, lemon grass slices, remaining shallots or onion, cucumber, carrots, some of the spring onions/scallions and some of the coriander/cilantro and torn mint leaves. Add the dressing.

4 **PILE** onto a deep serving dish and garnish with the remaining spring onion, coriander and mint leaves. (If this salad is to be eaten as part of a picnic, dress with just a third of the dressing and take the remainder with you to pour over at the last minute.)

Thanying Salad

Yum Thanying

Reputed to be a dish revered by the Thai royal family, this mixture of chicken and
vegetables folded into a sour, sweet and salty cucumber relish is certainly fit for a king!
This is a speciality from a famous restaurant in Bangkok, The Thanying.

**Serves 4 • Preparation time: 30 minutes
• Cooking time: 4 minutes**

¼ cucumber, halved, deseeded, then coarsely
   grated or diced
4 shallots or 1 small red onion, sliced
2–3 red chillies, deseeded and sliced
2 tbsp light or dark brown sugar
4 tbsp rice vinegar
freshly ground black pepper
200g/7oz long or green beans, trimmed
2 tsp sesame seeds, to garnish
55g/2oz/¹/₃ cup salted peanuts, finely crushed
375g/13oz cold cooked chicken, cut into
   fine strips
3 carrots, cut into matchsticks
115g/4oz/1 cup bean sprouts, brown tails
   removed if necessary
lettuce leaves, to garnish
6 coriander/cilantro stems, leaves chopped,
   to garnish

1 **PLACE** the grated or diced cucumber in a bowl. Pound the shallots or
onion and chillies to a paste using a pestle and mortar, then add the
sugar, vinegar and pepper. It should taste sour, sweet and salty.

2 **PLUNGE** the beans into a saucepan of boiling water for 2 minutes, then
drain and cut into pieces.

3 **WARM** a frying pan, then dry-fry the sesame seeds for 2 minutes until
golden, moving them all the time to avoid catching.

4 **TOSS** the cucumber and the pounded ingredients together with the
peanuts, then fold in the chicken strips, beans, carrots and bean sprouts
just before serving.

5 **TURN** onto a serving dish with some lettuce leaves and garnish with the
coriander/cilantro leaves and the toasted sesame seeds.

Squid Salad
Yum Pla Meuk

Rings or attractive curls of squid, stir-fried then marinated in herbs, chillies,
fresh lemon, fish sauce and a good helping of onion and garlic, served on
a bed of lettuce. You will find this dish on most restaurant menus.

**Serves 4 • Preparation time: 20–25 minutes
• Cooking time: 3 minutes**

450g/1lb ready-cleaned squid
juice of 1 large lemon
2 tbsp fish sauce
1 garlic clove, crushed
1 red chilli, deseeded and finely shredded
1 lemon grass stem, lower 6cm/2½in finely
    sliced
4 spring onions/scallions, white parts only,
    shredded
2 shallots, finely sliced
2–3 mint sprigs, leaves chopped
2 coriander/cilantro stems, leaves chopped
lettuce leaves, to garnish
4 lime leaves, finely shredded, to garnish
1 lemon, cut into 4 wedges, to serve

1 **PREPARE** the squid and cut into strips or rings (see page 19); keep the
tentacles to one side.

2 **HEAT** a wok, without any oil, toss in the squid rings or strips and
stir-fry for 2–3 minutes until the pieces of squid look cooked and are
curling. Lift out of the wok with a slotted spoon into a bowl. Repeat
with the tentacles.

3 **SPOON** the lemon juice, fish sauce, garlic, chilli and half the lemon grass
slices over the squid. Cover with cling film/plastic wrap and chill until
the salad is ready to serve.

4 **ADD** most of the spring onions/scallions to the fish salad with the
shallots just before serving, with some of the mint and coriander/cilantro
leaves scattered over.

5 **LINE** a serving dish with lettuce leaves, turn the well-mixed fish onto
this and garnish with the remaining lemon grass slices, mint and
coriander leaves and the shredded lime leaves. Provide lemon wedges
to squeeze over the dish.

Baby Corn and Sugar Snaps with Ginger and Garlic

Pad Yod Kao Pod Kab Khing

Vibrantly coloured vegetables with zingy ginger and garlic flavours, which can be cooked and served in double-quick time. The oyster sauce adds a gloss and sophistication to these simple vegetables.

Serves 4 • Preparation time: 6–8 minutes
• Cooking time: 5 minutes

4 garlic cloves, sliced
2.5cm/1in piece fresh root ginger, peeled and
   cut into matchsticks
½ onion, finely sliced
115g/4oz baby corn, cut in half at an angle
115g/4oz sugar snap peas
1 tbsp oyster sauce
1 tbsp fish sauce
2 tbsp sunflower oil
freshly ground black pepper

1 **ASSEMBLE** all the prepared vegetables next to the stove.

2 **BLEND** the oyster and fish sauces with 1 tbsp water in a bowl.

3 **HEAT** a wok before adding the oil. Allow to become hot, then toss in the garlic, ginger and onion, turning all the time so that the garlic does not brown and become bitter.

4 **ADD** the corn and sugar snap peas and toss well for 2 minutes, then pour in the sauce mixture. Cover with a lid and cook for 1 minute.

5 **TOP** with a little black pepper and serve on a warm serving dish.

Mixed Stir-fry Vegetables
Pad Pak Ruam Mitr

This deliciously crisp and colourful stir-fry makes the perfect accompaniment to any main dish, or could just be eaten on its own. Choose any vegetables you want, but aim for a good mix of colour and texture for the perfect result.

Serves 4 • Preparation time: 12 minutes • Cooking time: 5 minutes

450g/1lb mixed vegetables: broccoli, green beans, Brussels sprouts, carrots, cabbage, bean sprouts and/or spinach (any combination), trimmed and cut into bite-size pieces
2 tbsp fish sauce
2 tbsp oyster sauce
3 tbsp sunflower oil
2 garlic cloves, finely chopped
½ tsp sugar
freshly ground black pepper

1 **RINSE** and drain the vegetables. Set the cabbage, bean sprouts and/or spinach aside. Assemble all the vegetables by the stove.

2 **COMBINE** the fish and oyster sauces with 3 tbsp water in a small bowl.

3 **HEAT** a wok, add the oil and first fry the garlic without browning it too much.

4 **ADD** all the remaining vegetables, except for the cabbage, bean sprouts and/or spinach, then add the sugar and season with black pepper. Toss well, turning all the time to cook while retaining the crunchiness.

5 **ADD** the sauce mixture and the remaining vegetables. Reduce the heat, cover and cook for a further 2 minutes.

6 **SERVE** on a warm serving dish.

Stir-fry Broccoli and Carrots with Bean Curd and Peanuts

Pad Broc-co-li Kab Tofu

A simple vegetable dish is transformed into a vegetarian main meal with
the addition of some deep-fried bean curd and some lightly crushed peanuts.

Serves 4 • Preparation time: 8–10 minutes • Cooking time: 6 minutes

2 carrots, trimmed
280g/10oz broccoli, any tender stems cut into matchsticks, head divided into florets
1 tbsp fish sauce
1 tbsp oyster sauce
4 tbsp hot water or chicken or vegetable stock (see page 23)
3 tbsp sunflower oil
1 onion, cut into fine wedges
2.5cm/1in piece fresh root ginger, peeled and cut into matchsticks
freshly ground black pepper
115g/4oz fried bean curd cubes (optional)
25g/1oz/scant ¼ cup roasted peanuts, lightly crushed (optional)

1 **LAY** the carrots on a chopping/cutting board and make an angled cut along the length of each one, then another cut very close to make a "V" shape. Remove the strip and repeat the process two or three times around each carrot, then slice the carrots finely to make pretty flower shapes.

2 **PLUNGE** the broccoli into a saucepan of boiling water for 1 minute to turn it bright green. Drain immediately and rinse with cold water.

3 **BLEND** the fish and oyster sauces with the water or stock and set aside.

4 **HEAT** a wok and warm the oil. Fry the onion and ginger first without browning, then toss in the carrots and stir-fry over a high heat for 2 minutes. Add any tender broccoli stems and the florets. Keep turning over a high heat for 1 minute.

5 **POUR** in the sauce mixture and add some black pepper. Cover with a lid and steam for 1 minute. Add the bean curd at this stage, if using.

6 **SERVE** immediately, topped with the peanuts, if using.

Spicy Green Beans

Pad Ped Tou Kag

These beans are a rich vibrant colour and full of flavour and crispness.
The combination of the beans with aromatic curry paste and piquant
fish sauce creates a perfect vegetable dish for any Thai meal.

Serves 4 • Preparation time: 6–8 minutes
• Cooking time: 5 minutes

450g/1lb green or long beans, stalk end
  trimmed, and sliced into 5cm/2in pieces
3 tbsp sunflower oil
1 tbsp red curry paste (see page 24)
2 tbsp fish sauce
2 tbsp sugar

1 **PLUNGE** the beans into a saucepan of boiling water for 30 seconds, then drain and set aside.

2 **HEAT** a wok, add the oil and swirl it over the surface of the pan. Add the curry paste, then fry over a moderate heat until it changes colour and gives off a rich, fragrant aroma.

3 **ADD** the green beans and stir-fry until they are tender. Add the fish sauce, sugar and 125ml/4fl oz/½ cup boiling water and bring the mixture rapidly to the boil.

4 **TRANSFER** the cooked beans and sauce to a warm serving bowl and serve immediately.

Market Salad

Som Tam

A traditional salad of coarsely grated green papaya and tomato wedges mixed with green beans, fresh red chilli, lemon or lime juice, fish sauce and pounded dried prawns/shrimp. If green papaya is unavailable, use white cabbage or carrot.

Serves 4 • Preparation time: 15–20 minutes

450g/1lb green papaya, peeled, or white cabbage, shredded, and carrot, grated (optional)
1 red chilli, deseeded and sliced
1–2 long beans, sliced, or 6 green beans
1 tsp sugar
4 tbsp fish sauce
juice of 1 lemon or lime
25g/1oz dried prawns/shrimp, pounded to a powder using a pestle and mortar
2 tomatoes, cut into eighths, or 8 cherry tomatoes, cut in half
25–55g/1–2oz/¼–⅓ cup peanuts, crushed, to garnish
1–2 handfuls coriander/cilantro leaves, chopped, to garnish

1 **HOLD** the papaya in one hand and make deep slim cuts down into the flesh on one side with a very sharp knife. Then take off thin slices lengthways, leaving you with consistently sized shreds. Repeat all the way around on the other side.

2 **CRUSH** the chilli lightly with the beans and sugar using a pestle and mortar, then add the fish sauce and lemon or lime juice to taste.

3 **PLACE** the powdered dried prawns/shrimp, tomatoes, papaya or cabbage (or a mixture of cabbage and carrot) in a bowl, add the crushed chilli mixture and toss lightly.

4 **TURN** onzto a serving dish. Top with the peanuts and coriander/cilantro leaves just before serving.

Green Mango Salad

Yum Ma-Maung

A stunning layered salad of tart green mangoes, dried prawns/shrimp, toasted coconut and finely sliced red onion, on a lettuce-lined dish, drizzled with a spicy sweet and sour dressing and garnished with mint or coriander/cilantro leaves.

Serves 4 • Preparation time: 15 minutes • Cooking time: 1–2 minutes

2 large green mangoes or hard unripe yellow mangoes (these will give a sweeter result) or 1 pomelo or grapefruit
55g/2oz/½ cup desiccated/dried shredded coconut
soft lettuce
55g/2oz dried prawns/shrimp, pounded to a powder using a pestle and mortar
1 red onion, finely sliced
mint leaves, torn, or coriander/ cilantro leaves

FOR THE DRESSING
juice of 1 large lime or ½ lemon
3 tbsp fish sauce
1–2 bird's eye chillies (or more), deseeded and finely sliced
2 tbsp dark brown sugar

1 PEEL the mangoes with a potato peeler. Holding one in the palm of your hand, use a sharp knife to make lots of close cuts in the flesh of the mango. Now slice through the close cuts to make fine shards of flesh and repeat on the other side. Repeat with the second mango. If using a pomelo or grapefruit, remove the skin, divide into segments and remove the membranes, then chop lightly.

2 WARM a frying pan, then dry-fry the coconut for 1–2 minutes until golden, keeping it on the move to prevent it catching.

3 BLEND together the dressing ingredients in a small jug/pitcher.

4 LINE a serving dish with lettuce leaves, then layer up the mango, powdered prawns/shrimp, coconut and onion and some of the coriander/ cilantro or torn mint leaves.

5 POUR the dressing over the salad and garnish with the remaining coriander or torn mint. Toss before each person takes their helping.

Thai Mussaman Curry

Gaeng Mussaman

The tamarind juice adds contrasting sharpness in this hearty combination of spices, beef, nuts, shallots and potatoes. The spices in the Mussaman curry paste indicate the influence of Indian and Arab traders from centuries ago.

Serves 6 • Preparation time: 25 minutes • Cooking time: 2½ hours

1½ cans coconut milk (600ml/21fl oz/2½ cups)
1kg/2lb 4oz good-quality stewing or braising beef/chuck steak, trimmed and cut into 2.5cm/1in cubes
2 tbsp tamarind pulp
4 tbsp Mussaman curry paste (see page 25)
280g/10oz tiny new potatoes, cut in half if larger than bite-size
225g/8oz small onions or shallots
3 tbsp sunflower oil
55g/2oz/⅓ cup roasted peanuts
55g/2oz/¼ cup dark brown or palm (jaggery) sugar
juice of ½ lemon or lime
1 red chilli, sliced, to garnish

1 **RINSE** a casserole/Dutch oven or heavy saucepan with water – this helps to prevent the bottom of the pan catching during the slow cooking. Pour in the coconut milk and 325ml/11fl oz/1⅓ cups water and slowly bring to the boil.

2 **STIR** in the beef, return to the boil, then turn the heat down and simmer gently, uncovered, for 1½ hours, or until the beef is tender. Meanwhile, soak the tamarind pulp in 150ml/5fl oz/⅔ cup warm water for 10 minutes, then strain (see page 20).

3 **LIFT** the meat out with a slotted spoon into a separate container and reserve.

4 **REDUCE** the liquid in the pan by boiling for 5 minutes. Add the curry paste and cook for 3–4 minutes, stirring, to bring out the flavours.

5 **FRY** the potatoes and onions or shallots in the hot oil in a separate frying pan for 5 minutes until golden. Add to the spicy coconut sauce with the meat and the peanuts, and cook for 20–30 minutes.

6 **ADD** the strained tamarind juice, sugar and lemon or lime juice. Cook for a further 10 minutes before serving garnished with the sliced chilli. (Ideally, cook this the day before you need it, to let the flavours develop, and reheat for 1–1½ hours at 170°C/325°F/Gas 3 in a covered dish.)

Jungle Curry

Gaeng Pah

A rustic meal artfully cooked so that the beef is beautifully tender but the vegetables retain their natural crispness. This curry is so-called because the itinerant cook would have used whatever could be found to prepare the meal.

Serves 4 • Preparation time: 25 minutes • Cooking time: 1¾ hours

3 tbsp sunflower oil

3 tbsp red curry paste (see page 24)

700g/1½lb braising/chuck steak, cut into thin, even-size strips across the grain

3 tbsp fish sauce

3 pieces krachai, cut into matchsticks

175g/6oz long or green beans, cut into 2.5cm/1in lengths

175g/6oz egg-size white aubergines/eggplants, cut into quarters

115g/4oz baby corn, halved if liked

3 lime leaves, torn

1 tsp fresh green peppercorns (optional)

2–3 green chillies, deseeded, if liked, and sliced

2 sweet basil sprigs, leaves only

750ml/26fl oz/3¼ cups beef stock or 1 can beef consommé (300ml/10½fl oz/1¼ cups) made up with 425ml/115fl oz/1¾ cups water

2 tsp sugar

1 HEAT a wok and then add the oil. When hot, add the curry paste to taste and stir until it releases a rich aroma.

2 ADD the slices of beef and stir constantly until the meat changes colour. Add the fish sauce, then the krachai, vegetables, lime leaves, peppercorns, chillies and some of the basil leaves.

3 STIR in the stock and sugar and bring to the boil. Half-cover and simmer gently for 1–1½ hours, or until the beef is tender. Taste for seasoning and adjust if necessary. Garnish with the remaining basil leaves, then serve.

Northern Thai Curry with Pork and Ginger

Gaeng Hung Lay

A typical earthy-flavoured pork curry made using Hung Lay curry paste, sharp tamarind juice, turmeric, fish sauce and ginger, and garnished with pork crackling.

Serves 4–6 • Preparation time: 30 minutes, plus 1¼ hours soaking and marinating time • Cooking time: 1¼ hours

1 tbsp tamarind pulp
700g/1½lb pork, trimmed and cut into large pieces
3 tbsp Hung Lay curry paste (see page 25)
2 tsp ground turmeric
1 tsp five spice powder
2 tbsp brown or palm (jaggery) sugar
3 tbsp fish sauce
7.5cm/3in piece fresh root ginger, peeled and cut into matchsticks
3 shallots, sliced
4 garlic cloves, crushed
750ml/26fl oz/3¼ cups chicken stock (see page 23)
40g/1½oz pork crackling (see page 18), to garnish

1 **SOAK** the tamarind pulp in 4 tbsp warm water for 15 minutes, then strain (see page 20).

2 **COMBINE** the pork with the curry paste, turmeric, five spice powder, sugar, strained tamarind juice, fish sauce, one-third of the ginger, the shallots and garlic.

3 **MIX** well, then cover and leave in a cool place to marinate for 1 hour.

4 **WARM** a casserole/Dutch oven or wok. Turn in the marinated pork and stock. Bring to the boil, then reduce the heat to a simmer. Cover with the lid just slightly off centre and simmer over a low heat for 1¼ hours, or until the pork becomes tender.

5 **GARNISH** with pork crackling and the remaining ginger.

Green Chicken Curry

Gaeng Khiew Waan Gai

A huge favourite, almost the signature dish of Thai restaurants everywhere.
Here slices of chicken breast are cooked in the green curry paste and coconut sauce,
with torn lime leaves and fish sauce.

**Serves 4 • Preparation time: 15 minutes
• Cooking time: 12–15 minutes**

1 can coconut milk (400ml/14fl oz/1²/₃ cups)
3 tbsp green curry paste (see page 24)
2 boneless chicken breasts (175–200g/ 6–7oz
    each), cut into even-size strips
150ml/5 fl oz/²/₃ cup water or stock
2–3 tbsp fish sauce
1 tsp sugar
4–5 lime leaves, torn or finely shredded
100g/3½oz tiny pea aubergines/eggplants,
    stalks removed
1 small handful coriander/cilantro leaves,
    roughly chopped
1–2 sweet basil sprigs, leaves only, to garnish
1 small green and/or red chilli, deseeded and
    cut into strips, to garnish

1 **POUR** one-third of the can of coconut milk into a heated wok. Let it begin to bubble around the edges.

2 **STIR** in the curry paste and stir-fry for 2–3 minutes, stirring frequently, to bring out the full flavour.

3 **ADD** the chicken strips, keeping them separate. Turn them in the sauce in the wok until they are well coated.

4 **MIX** the remaining coconut milk with the water or stock plus 2 tbsp of the fish sauce and the sugar and add to the wok. Finally, add the lime leaves, aubergines/eggplants and the coriander/cilantro leaves.

5 **SIMMER** for 10 minutes, or until the chicken pieces are tender. Taste, and add more fish sauce, if liked.

6 **TRANSFER** to a warmed serving bowl and garnish with the basil leaves and strips of green or red chillies, or both.

Roast Duck Curry
Gaeng Phed Ped Yang

Delicious morsels of roast duck and crunchy, tart, pea aubergines/eggplants are added to
this curry sauce, which is based on the famous green curry paste and coconut milk
combination, to make one of the most famous of all Thai curries.

Serves 4–6 • Preparation time: 10 minutes
• Cooking time: 50 minutes, plus roasting time

1 duck (2.25kg/5lb) or 2 good-size duck
   breast portions
1 can coconut milk (400ml/14fl oz/1²/₃ cups)
1–2 tbsp green curry paste (see page 24)
4 lime leaves, torn
2 tbsp fish sauce
300ml/10½fl oz/1¼ cups stock or water
1 large red and 1 large green chilli , deseeded
   and sliced
200g/7oz pea aubergines/eggplants, stalks
   removed
3 tomatoes, quartered
2 sweet basil sprigs and coriander/cilantro
   stems, leaves only

1 **ROAST** the duck as suggested on the packaging. Allow to cool, then cut
into small pieces, discarding the backbone, any fat and other bony pieces.
Set aside. Alternatively, pan-fry or roast 2 duck breasts as suggested on
the packaging. Allow to cool, then slice finely.

2 **HEAT** a wok, then pour in one-third of the coconut milk and heat until
bubbling. Add the curry paste and stir over a moderate heat until the
mixture gives off a rich aroma.

3 **REDUCE** the heat and add the torn lime leaves and fish sauce to taste,
then stir in the duck meat and turn in the sauce until it is all thoroughly
coated with the spicy mixture.

4 **BLEND** the remaining coconut milk with the stock or water and add to
the curry. Stir, then add the chillies and pea aubergines/eggplants.

5 **COOK** for 30 minutes, then add the tomatoes, some of the basil
leaves and all the coriander/cilantro leaves. Bubble gently for a further
10 minutes, then serve, garnished with the remaining basil.

Red Chicken Curry

Gaeng Phed Gai

Small chicken joints blended with red curry paste, coconut milk and a dash or two of fish sauce. The whole dish is enhanced with crunchy bamboo shoots or earthy straw mushrooms and sweet basil leaves.

Serves 4 • Preparation time: 20 minutes • Cooking time: 45–50 minutes

1 can coconut milk (400ml/14fl oz/1²/₃ cups)
3 tbsp red curry paste (see page 24)
1.5kg/3lb 5oz chicken, jointed and each
    quarter divided into 2 or 4 portions, or 2–3
    boneless chicken breasts (175g/6oz each),
    cut into strips.
2–3 tbsp fish sauce
1 tsp sugar
4–5 lime leaves, torn or finely shredded
1 can sliced bamboo shoots (227g/8oz) or
    straw mushrooms (425g/15oz), drained
1–2 sweet basil sprigs, leaves only
1 red chilli, deseeded and finely sliced,
    to garnish

1 **HEAT** a wok, then pour in one-third of the coconut milk and heat until bubbling. Add the curry paste and stir-fry for 2–3 minutes over a moderate heat to bring out the flavour.

2 **ADD** the chicken portions or strips. Turn them in the sauce in the wok until they are well coated.

3 **MIX** the remaining coconut milk with 150ml/5fl oz/²/₃ cup water plus 2 tbsp of the fish sauce and the sugar and add to the wok. Finally, add the lime leaves and bamboo shoots or straw mushrooms.

4 **SIMMER** for 40–45 minutes if using chicken portions, or until they are tender. Simmer for only 10 minutes if using chicken strips. Taste, and add more fish sauce, if liked, and most of the basil.

5 **TRANSFER** to a warmed serving bowl and garnish with the remaining basil and the red chilli.

Prawn and Pineapple Curry
Gaeng Khau Goong

Prawns/shrimp take on a new identity when simmered in coconut milk and red curry paste,
hot with chilli, sweet and juicy with pineapple, salty with dried prawns/shrimp and
sharpened with tamarind juice – all the essential Thai flavours.

**Serves 4 • Preparation time: 12–15 minutes,
plus 10 minutes soaking time
• Cooking time: 12–15 minutes**

1 tsp tamarind pulp
1 can coconut milk (400ml/14fl oz/1²/₃ cups)
2 tbsp red curry paste (see page 24)
1 red and 1 green bird's eye chilli, deseeded
    and sliced
1 tbsp dried prawns/shrimp, pounded to a
    powder using a pestle and mortar
2 tbsp fish sauce
400g/14oz shelled tiger prawns/shrimp or same
    weight white fish or salmon, skinned,
    boned and cut into bite-size pieces
6–8 cherry tomatoes, halved if liked
1 thick slice fresh or canned pineapple,
    cut into small pieces
1 basil sprig, leaves only

1 **SOAK** the tamarind pulp in 3 tbsp warm water for 10 minutes, then
strain (see page 20).

2 **HEAT** a wok, then pour in one-third of the coconut milk and heat until
bubbling. Add the curry paste and stir over a moderate heat to bring out
the flavour.

3 **ADD** the remaining coconut milk plus 150ml/5fl oz/²/₃ cup warm water,
chillies, powdered prawns/shrimp, fish sauce and strained tamarind juice.
Bring slowly to the boil, then simmer for 8–10 minutes.

4 **ADD** the fresh prawns/shrimp, or fish if using, tomatoes and pineapple.
Cook gently for 3–4 minutes, then add most of the basil leaves at the
last moment.

5 **TRANSFER** to a warmed bowl and scatter with the remaining basil.

Khun Nan's Steamed Fish Curry
Hor Mok Pla

Traditionally this curry would have been cooked in a banana leaf cup,
which does add a special flavour and looks sensational too.

**Serves 4 • Preparation time: 20 minutes
• Cooking time: 15 minutes**

1 can coconut milk (400ml/14fl oz/1²/₃ cups)
2 tbsp red curry paste (see page 24)
2 tbsp fish sauce
1 egg, beaten
25g/1oz/¼ cup rice flour
1 tsp sugar
400g/14oz cod, haddock or salmon fillet
    or other fish of your choice, skinned and
    cut into bite-size pieces, or raw tiger
    prawns/shrimp, cut in half
6 lime leaves, very finely shredded
2 tsp sunflower oil (optional)
4 banana cups (optional)
2 Chinese cabbage leaves, torn into pieces
2 sweet basil sprigs, leaves only, torn
1 red chilli, sliced

1 **PUT** the coconut milk (reserving 2 tbsp for the garnish), curry paste, fish sauce, beaten egg, rice flour and sugar in a bowl and blend to a smooth, thick batter. Add the fish pieces and 4 of the lime leaves, reserving the rest for the garnish.

2 **BRUSH** four large ramekins lightly with oil or make four banana cups, if using (see page 26).

3 **PLACE** a piece of Chinese cabbage in the base of each ramekin. Divide the fish mixture between them and top with the torn basil leaves and some of the slices of chilli.

4 **PLACE** the ramekins in a large, wide frying pan with boiling water to come halfway up their sides. Cover and steam for 15 minutes until the tops are just set (a skewer will come out clean). Alternatively, steam for the same time on a large bamboo steaming tray set over a wok and covered; cook in a water bath in the microwave on full power, covered loosely with cling film/plastic wrap (8 minutes cooking time and 2 minutes resting); or cook in an electric steamer for 15 minutes. If using banana cups, fill at the last minute to avoid any possibility of leaking and use crumpled foil to keep the cups steady.

5 **SERVE** hot, garnished with the reserved coconut milk, reserved shredded lime leaves and reserved chilli slices.

Mixed Vegetable Curry

Gaeng Kari Pak

Perfectly prepared vegetables, gently cooked in coconut milk and combined with curry paste. Use baby corn, white aubergines/eggplants cut into quarters, carrots cut into fine slices and courgettes/zucchini either sliced or cut into neat chunks.

Serves 4–6 • Preparation time: 20 minutes • Cooking time: 12–15 minutes

1 can coconut milk (400ml/14fl oz/1²/₃ cups)
2 tbsp red or green curry paste (see page 24)
2cm/¾in piece turmeric root or 2 tsp ground turmeric
300ml/10½fl oz/1¼ cups vegetable stock (see page 23)
600g/1lb 5oz vegetables: baby corn, halved, white aubergines/eggplants, quartered, carrots, cut into batons, and courgettes/zucchini, sliced
2 tbsp fish sauce
3 lime leaves, finely shredded
1 basil sprig and 1 coriander/cilantro stem, leaves only

1 **HEAT** a wok, then pour in one-third of the coconut milk and heat until bubbling. Add the curry paste and stir over a moderate heat to bring out the flavour.

2 **PEEL** the piece of turmeric, if using, wearing gloves to protect against staining, then pound it to a paste using a pestle and mortar. Add this or the ground turmeric to the wok along with the remaining coconut milk and vegetable stock, then bring to the boil.

3 **ADD** the prepared vegetables, return to a gentle boil, stirring all the time. Add the fish sauce and some of the lime, basil and coriander/cilantro leaves.

4 **SIMMER** gently, testing a piece of vegetable now and then, until the vegetables are just cooked but the corn and carrots are still slightly crunchy. Taste and adjust the seasoning, adding more fish sauce if wanted.

5 **SERVE** in a hot bowl, garnished with the remaining leaves.

Beef with Broccoli and Oyster Sauce
Neau Pad Pak Nammaun Hoy

The tenderest beef fillet/filet mignon and the brightest green broccoli make perfect partners. Add a dash of oyster sauce, some garlic, spring onions/scallions and a generous amount of seasoning and you have a stunning creation.

Serves 4 • Preparation time: 10 minutes • Cooking time: 7–8 minutes

200g/7oz broccoli, cut into tiny florets
4 tbsp sunflower oil
400g/14oz beef fillet/filet mignon, sliced into neat, even-size pieces
2 garlic cloves, crushed
2 tbsp oyster sauce
5 tbsp chicken stock (see page 23)
salt and freshly ground black pepper
5 spring onions/scallions, cut into short lengths

1 **BRING** a pan of boiling water to the boil and plunge the broccoli florets in for 1 minute, then drain and rinse with cold water.

2 **HEAT** a wok, add the oil and, when very hot, toss in the beef and garlic. Stir-fry for 4 minutes until the meat has changed colour and looks tender.

3 **ADD** the blanched broccoli florets, oyster sauce and the stock. Cover and cook over a high heat for 1–2 minutes, stirring once or twice.

4 **TASTE** for seasoning, toss in the spring onions/scallions and stir-fry for a few more seconds.

5 **SERVE** immediately on a hot serving dish.

Stir-fry Noodles with Pork or Beef
Guay Tiew Pad Si-Ew

Rice noodles tossed with stir-fried pork or beef fillet/filet mignon, Chinese leaves, Napa cabbage and scrambled egg, all enhanced with soy and crushed yellow bean sauces and a handful of spring onions/scallions – an unbelievable gastronomic experience.

Serves 4 • Preparation time: 10 minutes • Cooking time: 6–8 minutes

400g/14oz rice noodles (guay tiew)
2 tbsp sunflower oil
2 garlic cloves, crushed
225g/8oz pork or beef fillet/filet mignon, cut into thin strips
1 large egg, beaten
6 Chinese/Nappa cabbage leaves or any green leaves, trimmed and chopped into bite-size pieces
1 tsp dark soy sauce
1 tbsp light soy sauce
1 tbsp crushed yellow bean sauce
1 tsp sugar
salt and freshly ground black pepper
4 spring onions/scallions, cut into neat lengths

1 **SEPARATE** the noodles and plunge into boiling water. Drain, then slice the folded noodles into ribbons.

2 **ASSEMBLE** the remaining ingredients.

3 **HEAT** a wok, add the oil and, when hot, fry the garlic until turning golden, then add the beef or pork and toss all the time until the meat changes colour and is cooked. This will take just a couple of minutes for beef and a little longer for pork.

4 **ADD** the egg to the wok and stir until it just begins to scramble, then add the Chinese or other leaves. Cook for only a few seconds, then add the rice noodles.

5 **TOSS** well and then add the soy sauces, crushed yellow bean sauce and sugar. Mix well and taste for seasoning. Add most of the spring onions/ scallions.

6 **TURN** into a warmed serving bowl and garnish with the remaining spring onions. Serve immediately.

Stir-fry Pork and Prawns with Wing Beans
Moo Lae Goong Pad Tao

A fabulous mixture of tender pork tossed in a red curry paste with bright green wing beans and fresh prawns/shrimp moistened with fish sauce and sweetened to just the right degree.

Serves 4 • Preparation time: 8–10 minutes • Cooking time: 10 minutes

250g/9oz wing or green beans, cut into
    2.5cm/1in lengths
4 tbsp sunflower oil
2 tbsp red curry paste (see page 24)
225g/8oz boneless pork fillet, thinly sliced
3–4 tbsp hot water
4 tbsp fish sauce
115g/4oz/½ cup shelled cooked prawns/shrimp
1 tbsp light brown sugar
freshly ground black pepper

1 **PLUNGE** the beans into boiling water for 2 minutes, then drain, rinse with cold water and drain again.

2 **ASSEMBLE** the remaining ingredients.

3 **HEAT** a wok, add the oil and, when hot, stir-fry the curry paste to bring out the flavour. Add the pork slices and cook until the pork changes colour. Thin slices will cook quite quickly.

4 **ADD** the hot water, fish sauce, prawns/shrimp and beans. Stir well, then add the sugar and black pepper. Taste and adjust the seasoning, then serve at once.

Stir-fry Chilli Pork
Moo Pad Prik

A quick and sumptuous dish of thinly sliced pork, tossed with garlic, chilli and spring onions/scallions, moistened with Thai fish sauce and served piping hot. It is important that the pork is sliced very thinly so that it will cook quickly.

Serves 4 • Preparation time: 10 minutes • Cooking time: 8 minutes

4 tbsp sunflower oil
400g/14oz boneless pork fillet, trimmed and
   sliced into neat, even-size pieces
1 small onion, finely sliced
2 garlic cloves, crushed
1–2 red chillies, deseeded and finely sliced
4 spring onions/scallions, cut into
   short lengths
4 tbsp stock or water
1 tbsp fish sauce
freshly ground black pepper

1 **ASSEMBLE** all the ingredients.

2 **HEAT** a wok, add the oil and, when hot, toss in the pork, onion and garlic. Stir-fry for 5–6 minutes until the pork changes colour and is tender.

3 **ADD** the remaining ingredients and quickly toss together. Taste for seasoning and serve immediately on a hot dish.

Stir-fry Chicken with Basil Leaves
Gai Pad Bai Kaprow

The chicken is wonderfully perfumed with fresh basil leaves, but the bird's eye chillies add dragon-like fire. To be truly authentic, the fiendishly hot chillies should be simply crushed, but you may prefer to remove some of the seeds.

Serves 4 • Preparation time: 12–15 minutes • Cooking time: 8 minutes

1 small, finger-length red chilli, to garnish
4 tbsp sunflower oil
2 chicken breasts (175–200g/6–7oz each), boned and skinned and cut into neat, bite-size pieces
2 garlic cloves, crushed
1 onion, finely sliced
15 holy basil leaves
2–3 bird's eye chillies, deseeded, if liked, and sliced or crushed
2 tbsp fish sauce
1 tsp light brown sugar

1 **MAKE** a chilli flower following the instructions on page 26, leaving it to soak in iced water while you prepare and cook the stir-fry.

2 **ASSEMBLE** all the ingredients.

3 **HEAT** a wok, add half the oil and, when hot, stir-fry the chicken pieces and garlic together. Stir-fry until the chicken pieces change colour and are cooked through. Remove from the wok and keep warm.

4 **WIPE** the wok with paper towels, then add the remaining oil and stir-fry the onion with most of the basil leaves and chillies for 3 minutes.

5 **RETURN** the chicken to the wok, add the fish sauce and sugar and mix well.

6 **TURN** onto a hot serving dish and garnish with the chilli flower and remaining basil leaves. Serve at once.

Stir-fry Duck Breasts with Ginger and Black Bean Sauce

Ped Pad Khing

Another winning combination – fresh root ginger, black bean sauce, garlic and Chinese mushrooms stir-fried with juicy slices of duck breast and spring onions/scallions and served garnished with shreds of crispy duck skin.

Serves 4 • Preparation time: 15 minutes • Cooking time: 8 minutes, plus 1 hour rendering time

2 boneless duck breasts (280–325g/10–11½oz each), finely sliced
6 Chinese mushrooms
3 tbsp sunflower oil or duck fat (optional)
1 garlic clove, crushed
2.5cm/1in piece fresh root ginger, peeled and shredded
1 small onion, sliced
1–2 tbsp black bean sauce
1 tsp sugar
freshly ground black pepper
4 spring onions/scallions, cut into short lengths

1 **PREHEAT** the oven to 180°C/350°F/Gas 4.

2 **TRIM** the skin from the duck breasts, if liked, and render down in an ovenproof dish in the oven for about 1 hour until all the fat has melted and the skin is crisp. Reserve the duck fat for cooking the meat, if wanted, and slice the crisp skin into fine strips for the garnish. Meanwhile, soak the Chinese mushrooms in warm water for 20–30 minutes.

3 **ASSEMBLE** all the remaining ingredients.

4 **DRAIN** the mushrooms, reserving 2–3 tbsp of the soaking liquid. Discard the stalks and slice the mushroom caps finely.

5 **HEAT** the oil or duck fat in a wok and, when hot, add the duck slices, garlic and ginger and toss constantly until the duck meat changes colour and is tender.

6 **ADD** the onion, mushrooms, black bean sauce, sugar and the mushroom soaking liquid. Toss well and taste for seasoning.

7 **ADD** the spring onions/scallions and turn out immediately onto a hot serving dish. Serve scattered with the crispy skin slices, if liked.

Stir-fry Chicken with Cashew Nuts

Gai Pad Mamaung Himmaparn

A favourite combination of sweet, almost creamy, cashews roasted to
bring out their nuttiness and stir-fried with the tenderest chicken breasts,
subtly flavoured with fish and oyster sauces and just a hint of garlic.

**Serves 4 • Preparation time: 12–15 minutes
• Cooking time: 6 minutes**

3 tbsp sunflower oil
2 skinless chicken breasts (225g/8oz each),
    sliced into neat, even-size strips
1 garlic clove, crushed
1 onion, finely sliced
55g/2oz/generous ¹⁄₃ cup roasted cashew nuts,
    halved lengthways
3 tbsp fish sauce
1 tbsp oyster sauce
4 spring onions/scallions, cut into
    short lengths
salt and freshly ground black pepper

1 **ASSEMBLE** all the ingredients.

2 **HEAT** a wok, add the oil and, when hot, toss in the chicken and
garlic and stir-fry for 3–4 minutes until the chicken pieces are tender
and golden.

3 **ADD** the remaining ingredients. Cook for only 1 minute, then taste for
seasoning and serve on a hot serving dish.

Sweet and Sour Chicken
Pad Priew-Waan Gai

Nothing like Chinese sweet and sour dishes, here the chicken is stir-fried gently then simmered with colourful red and green vegetables, flavoured with tomato, sharpened with rice vinegar and sweetened with sugar to form a rich-tasting sauce.

Serves 4 • Preparation time: 15 minutes • Cooking time: 8–10 minutes

4 tbsp sunflower oil
2 skinless chicken breasts (225g/8oz each), sliced into neat, even-size strips
¼ small onion, finely sliced
¼ each red and green pepper, finely sliced
2.5cm/1in piece cucumber, finely sliced
4 cherry tomatoes, halved
4 spring onions/scallions, cut into short lengths
1 tsp tomato purée/paste
1 tbsp rice vinegar
1 tbsp fish sauce
1 tsp sugar
4 tbsp chicken stock (see page 23) (optional)
freshly ground black pepper
coriander/cilantro leaves, to garnish

1 **ASSEMBLE** all the ingredients.

2 **HEAT** a wok, add the oil and, when hot, stir-fry the chicken pieces for 3–5 minutes until they change colour and are tender.

3 **ADD** all the other ingredients along with the stock, if needed, to make a sauce. Cook for 3–4 minutes. Taste and adjust the seasoning.

4 **SERVE** on a warm dish garnished with coriander/cilantro leaves.

Stir-fry Squid with Garlic
Pla Meuk Kratiem Prikthai

As the attractively prepared squid is stir-fried with garlic, coriander/cilantro, ground black pepper and oyster sauce, the juices give off a heady aroma.

Serves 4 • Preparation time: 20 minutes • Cooking time: 5 minutes

450g/1lb ready-cleaned squid
2 tbsp sunflower oil
1–2 garlic cloves, crushed
2 coriander/cilantro stems, stalks pounded
½ tsp freshly ground black pepper
1 tbsp oyster sauce
6 spring onions/scallions, cut into 2.5cm/1in lengths

1 **PREPARE** the squid and cut any tiny squid into rings and the larger ones into strips (see page 19). Do not discard the tentacles, which are usually tucked into each ready-cleaned squid – add them to the recipe.

2 **ASSEMBLE** all the ingredients.

3 **HEAT** a wok, add the oil and, when hot, quickly fry the garlic and pounded coriander/cilantro stalks (reserving the leaves for the garnish) to bring out the flavour.

4 **KEEP** the wok over a high heat, then add the squid and tentacles. Stir-fry quickly for 2–3 minutes.

5 **ADD** the pepper and oyster sauce and finally the spring onions/scallions.

6 **TURN** onto a hot serving dish and serve garnished with the reserved coriander leaves.

Stir-fry Scallops with Chilli and Basil Leaves

Hoy Shell Pad Bai Kaprow

Scallops stir-fried with onion, chilli, basil and fish sauce create a sensational dish.
Scallops are best cooked briefly, and so are highly suited to a stir-fry.

Serves 3–4 • Preparation time: 10 minutes
• Cooking time: 2–3 minutes

6–8 large scallops or about 450g/1lb
    queen scallops
3 tbsp sunflower oil
½ onion, finely sliced
1 large red or green chilli, deseeded and
    finely sliced
2 holy basil sprigs, leaves only
4 spring onions/scallions, cut into
    short lengths
2 tbsp fish sauce
1 tsp sugar
freshly ground black pepper

1 **CUT** the large scallops horizontally through the centre to make 2 even-size round shapes. Remove the black thread from the smaller queen scallops and leave whole. Place on paper towels to drain any excess moisture.

2 **ASSEMBLE** all the other ingredients. When ready to cook, heat a wok, add the oil and, when hot, toss in the scallops and stir-fry for 1 minute.

3 **PUSH** the scallops to one side, then add the onion to the wok with the chilli and basil leaves. Keep tossing, then add the spring onions/scallions, fish sauce, sugar and pepper.

4 **TASTE** and adjust the seasoning, then serve immediately on a hot serving dish.

Stir-fry Green Vegetables with Yellow Bean Sauce

Pat Pak Boong Fai Daeng

Oriental greens stir-fried with a glorious mix of crushed yellow bean sauce, garlic and chillies. If you cannot buy pak boong, baby spinach makes a perfect substitute. Alternatively, use a combination of pak choi/bok choy and Savoy cabbage.

Serves 4 • Preparation time: 5 minutes • Cooking time: 3–4 minutes

1–2 chillies, deseeded and finely chopped
3 tbsp crushed yellow bean sauce
1 garlic clove, crushed
1 tbsp sugar
3 tbsp sunflower oil
400g/14oz pak boong or young spinach, or pak choi/bok choy, leaves used whole and white stalks cut into bite-size pieces, and Savoy cabbage, leaves torn

1 **PLACE** the chopped chillies, crushed yellow bean sauce, garlic and sugar in a bowl.

2 **HEAT** a wok, add the oil and, when hot, toss in the spicy sauce and the green vegetables together. Stir-fry for 3–4 minutes.

3 **TURN** onto a hot plate and serve at once.

Stir-fry Long Beans, Tomatoes and Chinese Leaves

Pad Tur Fak Yao, Makeur Thed Kab Kana

A stunningly attractive combination of colours, textures and oriental flavours make this a sumptuous stir-fry. Long beans, or yard beans as they are called in Malaysia, are very crunchy when young and add a lovely bite to this dish.

Serves 4 • Preparation time: 8 minutes • Cooking time: 3–4 minutes

3 tbsp sunflower oil
1 garlic clove, crushed
225g/8oz long or green beans, cut into 4cm/1½in lengths
2 large tomatoes, cut into eighths, or 8 cherry tomatoes
4 Chinese/Napa cabbage leaves, cut into 5cm/2in diamond-shaped pieces
1 tbsp light soy sauce
1 tbsp oyster sauce
1 tsp sugar
freshly ground black pepper

1 **ASSEMBLE** all the ingredients.

2 **HEAT** a wok over a medium heat, then add the oil and, when hot, stir-fry the garlic without browning.

3 **ADD** the beans immediately and toss well for 30 seconds, then add the tomatoes and Chinese/Napa cabbage leaves, stirring all the time.

4 **ADD** the soy and oyster sauces, sugar and pepper to taste. Cook for 1 minute, then serve at once so that the vegetables remain crisp.

Stuffed Omelettes

Kai Yat Sai

Kai yat sai is commonly served as a midday lunch dish and can be bought from stalls and cafés. Rarely found on restaurant menus, these omelettes are ideal for people in a hurry.

Serves 2–4 • Preparation time: 12–15 minutes • Cooking time: 15 minutes

3 garlic cloves, chopped
8 black peppercorns
6 coriander/cilantro stems
4 tbsp sunflower oil
115g/4oz minced/ground pork
1 onion, chopped
140g/5oz sugar snap peas or mangetout/snow peas, finely sliced
1 tomato, deseeded and chopped
1 tsp sugar
6 large eggs
1 tbsp fish sauce

1 **POUND** the garlic, peppercorns and coriander/cilantro roots and stalks (reserve the leaves for the garnish) to a juicy paste using a pestle and mortar.

2 **HEAT** half the oil in a warmed wok. Fry the paste, which will give off a rich aroma. Immediately add the pork and stir-fry until it changes colour.

3 **ADD** the onion, sugar snap peas or mangetout/snow peas and tomato, stir-frying for 1 minute between each addition, then stir in the sugar and set the wok aside.

4 **BEAT** the eggs and fish sauce together in a bowl. Heat half the remaining oil in a large frying pan over a medium heat.

5 **POUR** in half the eggs and tilt the pan until the surface is evenly coated. Keep lifting the mixture from the edges of the pan so that the raw egg mixture moves there and becomes cooked. When the omelette is cooked on one side but still creamy on top, spoon half the pork mixture down the centre of the omelette. Fold both sides over the filling, then slide the omelette onto a warmed plate. Keep warm.

6 **REPEAT** the process with the remaining ingredients to make a second omelette. Cut both omelettes in half and garnish with the coriander leaves.

Sweet and Sour Fish

Pla Priew-Waan

Whole red mullet, snapper or sea bass crisp-fried then served smothered in a rich sweet
and sour sauce with the fragrance of ginger and the flavour of Chinese mushrooms,
garnished with pineapple, shredded chillies and coriander/cilantro.

**Serves 2–4 • Preparation time: 15 minutes
• Cooking time: 15–20 minutes**

4 Chinese mushrooms
1 whole red mullet, snapper or sea bass
   (700g/1½lb), cleaned and scaled
1 tbsp seasoned flour
300ml/10½fl oz/1¼ cups sunflower oil
1 garlic clove, crushed
1 onion, finely sliced
1cm/½in piece fresh root ginger, peeled and
   finely shredded
2 tbsp rice vinegar
5 tbsp tomato ketchup
2 tbsp fish sauce
1 tsp cornflour/cornstarch
1–2 chillies, deseeded and finely sliced,
   to garnish
1–2 slices pineapple, cut into wedges, to
   garnish
coriander/cilantro leaves, to garnish

1 **SOAK** the Chinese mushrooms in warm water for 20–30 minutes, then
drain. Meanwhile, rinse the fish and dry well with paper towels. Coat in
the seasoned flour and, depending on the size of the frying pan, either
leave whole or remove the head to make it fit the pan, cook separately,
then push together to serve. If you choose a very large fish,
it can be cut in half, cooked and reassembled for serving.

2 **POUR** the oil into a frying pan so that it is about 2.5cm/1in deep and
cook the fish for 5–7 minutes on each side, or until cooked through.
Drain on paper towels and keep warm.

3 **SPOON** the remainder of the oil from cooking the fish into a clean
frying pan. Fry the garlic, onion and ginger to bring out the flavours.

4 **BLEND** the vinegar, tomato ketchup and fish sauce together with
200ml/7fl oz/scant 1 cup water and pour into the pan. Discard the
mushroom stalks, slice the caps finely and add to the pan, then cook
for 3–4 minutes.

5 **BLEND** the cornflour/cornstarch to a paste with 1 tbsp water, then stir
into the sauce to thicken.

6 **POUR** the sauce over the fish and serve garnished with the chillies,
pineapple and coriander/cilantro.

Fried Whole Fish with Tamarind Sauce

Pla Jien

The sharpness of tamarind juice offsets the sweetness of whole fried snapper, bream or sea bass and is complemented by the flavours of ginger, chillies and soy sauce.

Serves 2–4 • Preparation time: 20 minutes • Cooking time: 20 minutes

1 whole red snapper, sea bass or bream (650g/1lb 7oz), cleaned and scaled
2 tbsp seasoned cornflour/cornstarch
300ml/10½fl oz/1¼ cups sunflower oil

FOR THE TAMARIND SAUCE
25g/1oz tamarind pulp
2–3 garlic cloves, chopped
4–6 spring onions/scallions, white parts only, cut into short lengths
1cm/½in piece fresh root ginger, peeled and finely shredded
1 tbsp soy sauce
1–2 tbsp dark brown sugar
1–2 tbsp fish sauce
1–2 red chillies, deseeded and shredded, to garnish

1 **SOAK** the tamarind pulp in 150ml/5fl oz/⅔ cup warm water for 10 minutes, then strain (see page 20).

2 **RINSE** the fish and dry well with paper towels. Coat in the seasoned cornflour/cornstarch and, depending on the size of the frying pan, either leave whole or remove the head to make it fit the pan, cook separately, then push together to serve. If you choose a very large fish, it can be cut in half, cooked and reassembled for serving.

3 **POUR** the oil into a frying pan so that it is about 2.5cm/1in deep, and cook the fish for 5–7 minutes on each side, or until cooked through. Drain on paper towels and keep warm.

4 **FRY** the garlic in 2 tbsp of the oil from cooking the fish. Add the spring onions/scallions and ginger. Keep moving the ingredients around so that they do not brown.

5 **ADD** the soy sauce, sugar, fish sauce and tamarind juice, tasting until you have the right balance of sweet, sour and salty flavours.

6 **POUR** this sauce over the fish and serve garnished with the chillies.

Fried Bean Curd with Peanut Sauce and Cucumber Salad

Tao-Hoo Tawd

Slices of soft bean curd, carefully fried in garlic-flavoured oil, then bathed in a rich spicy peanut sauce, garnished with crushed peanuts and coriander/cilantro, and served with a deceptively spicy cucumber salad and prawn crackers/shrimp chips.

Serves 4 • Preparation time: 20 minutes • Cooking time: 10 minutes

4 tbsp sunflower oil
1 garlic clove, crushed
2 blocks fresh bean curd (115g/4oz total
   weight), drained, cut in half and sliced
1 recipe quantity peanut sauce (see page 28)
coriander/cilantro leaves, to garnish
prawn crackers/shrimp chips
   (see page 53), to serve

FOR THE CUCUMBER SALAD
½ cucumber, halved, deseeded and
   thinly sliced
6 shallots or 1 small red onion, finely sliced
3–4 tbsp basic dipping sauce or sweet chilli
   dipping sauce (see page 27)
1 red chilli, deseeded and finely sliced,
   to garnish
25g/1oz/scant ¼ cup peanuts, crushed,
   to garnish
sweet basil or coriander/cilantro leaves,
   to garnish
sea salt

1 **PREPARE** the cucumber salad. Salt the cucumber, then rinse and drain. Place in a serving dish with the shallots or red onion and spoon over the dipping sauce. Cover with cling film/plastic wrap and chill until required.

2 **HEAT** the oil in a wok and fry the garlic over a gentle heat, then fry the bean curd slices on both sides with care so that they do not break up. Drain well on crumpled paper towels.

3 **ARRANGE** the bean curd on a serving platter and pour over the hot peanut sauce. Garnish with coriander/cilantro leaves.

4 **TOP** the cucumber salad with the sliced chilli, peanuts and basil or coriander leaves. Serve the bean curd with the salad and prawn crackers/shrimp chips.

Deep-fried Noodles with Sweet and Savoury Sauce

Mee Krob

Serves 4 • Preparation time: 15 minutes • Cooking time: 20 minutes

2 eggs, beaten with 2 tbsp water
salt and freshly ground black pepper
6 tbsp sunflower oil, plus extra for deep-frying
4 shallots or 1 red onion, sliced, to garnish
55g/2oz dried prawns/shrimp, to garnish
175g/6oz fresh bean curd, cut into small cubes
1 cooked chicken breast, cut into thin strips
2 tbsp tomato purée/paste
1 tbsp rice vinegar
1 tsp salt
55g/2oz/¼ cup sugar
175g/6oz rice vermicelli noodles
115g/4oz/generous 1 cup bean sprouts, to garnish
2 spring onions/scallions, shredded, to garnish
2 red chillies, deseeded and sliced, to garnish
coriander/cilantro leaves, to garnish

1 **SEASON** the beaten egg. Heat a wok or frying pan and add 2 tbsp of the oil. Pour in the beaten egg and make an omelette. Turn onto a plate, roll into a sausage shape and allow to cool, then cut into neat pieces. Set aside for a garnish.

2 **ADD** the remaining 4 tbsp of the oil to the wok and fry the shallots or onion until golden, then drain on paper towels. Add the dried prawns/shrimp to the same oil and fry until crisp, then drain.

3 **POUR** the oil into a bowl, discard the sediment, then return the oil to the wok. Fry the bean curd until just colouring, then drain on paper towels. Add the chicken, tomato purée/paste, vinegar, salt, sugar and 125ml/4fl oz/½ cup water to the pan and cook to a glossy tomato sauce. Pour into a bowl and set aside. Clean the wok ready for the noodles.

4 **HEAT** the oil for deep-frying in the wok to 190°C/375°F no more than 30 minutes before serving. Crush the noodles lightly in a plastic bag.

5 **FRY** handfuls of the noodles very briefly – they will puff up and become crisp almost as soon as they are dropped into the hot oil. Remove at once before they take on any colour. Drain on paper towels.

6 **PLACE** the noodles in a large bowl and add the warmed sauce. Mix well, finally adding the fried bean curd. Turn onto a serving dish.

7 **GARNISH** the edge with the bean sprouts, omelette and spring onions/scallions. Scatter the top with the shallots or onion, dried prawns, chillies and coriander/cilantro.

Spiced Aubergine with Yellow Bean Sauce

Makua Pat Prik

Almost a meal in itself, this rich assembly of jewel-like vegetables
is a winner whether served hot, warm or cold.

**Serves 4 • Preparation time: 12–15 minutes
• Cooking time: 7–8 minutes**

3 tbsp sunflower oil

1–2 garlic cloves, crushed

2 red or green chillies, deseeded and
finely sliced

280g/10oz purple aubergine/eggplant, cut
into quarters lengthways, then sliced at
an angle

4 tbsp chicken or vegetable stock
(see page 23)

1 pepper, deseeded and cut into diamonds

2 tbsp crushed yellow bean sauce

1 tbsp light soy sauce

1 tsp sugar

1 sweet basil sprig, leaves only, to garnish

1 HEAT a wok, add the oil and, when hot, fry the garlic and most of the
chillies over a gentle heat until just softening.

2 ADD the aubergine/eggplant pieces and keep turning, then pour in the
stock. Turn all the time until the aubergine pieces are softening, then add
the pepper.

3 BLEND together the crushed yellow bean sauce, soy sauce and sugar. Add
to the wok. Stir gently, then cover and cook for a further 3 minutes over a
gentle heat. Taste for seasoning.

4 TURN into a warmed serving bowl, garnish with the reserved chillies and
lots of basil leaves. Serve hot.

Steamed Mussels with Lemon Grass and Basil

Hoy Malangpoo Neung

The most fragrant mussels you will ever eat – steamed in a wok with lemon grass, sweet basil and lime leaves and served with a stunning chilli fish sauce.

Serves 4 • Preparation time: 25–30 minutes • Cooking time: 5–6 minutes

1kg/2lb 4oz mussels
4 lemon grass stems, bruised
3 lime leaves, torn
4 sweet basil sprigs, leaves only

FOR THE CHILLI FISH SAUCE
juice of 1 large lemon
2 garlic cloves, crushed
4–6 bird's eye chillies, deseeded if wished, then chopped or pounded
3 tbsp fish sauce
2 tsp sugar

1 **SCRUB** each mussel carefully and remove any beards. Discard any with broken shells or those that are already open. Keep in a large container covered with water in the refrigerator until required.

2 **BLEND** all the sauce ingredients together in a bowl and set aside.

3 **LINE** the base of a wok or a steamer that is large enough to cook all the mussels with the bruised lemon grass stems, torn lime leaves and most of the basil leaves.

4 **HEAT** the wok, add the mussels and keep over a high heat. Pour in 300ml/10½fl oz/1¼ cups boiling water. Cover closely and steam for about 5 minutes or until the shells are open. Discard any that do not open in this time.

5 **SPOON** the mussels onto serving plates. Discard the flavouring herbs using a slotted spoon so that the juices remain in the wok.

6 **REHEAT** the juices until hot and add the prepared chilli fish sauce. Cook briefly, then spoon over the mussels on the serving plates and scatter over the remaining basil leaves to garnish.

Steamed Whole Fish with Preserved Plums in Banana Leaf Parcel

Pla Neung Bouy

Carp or sea bream flavoured with a heady mixture of chopped preserved plums, ginger, peppers, onions and typical Thai sauces, steamed almost to melting moistness and garnished with spring onions/scallions and coriander/cilantro.

Serves 2–4 • Preparation time: 10 minutes • Cooking time: 10–15 minutes

1 whole carp or sea bream (425g/15oz), cleaned, or fillets if preferred
1 banana leaf
2 tbsp sunflower oil, plus extra for oiling
3 preserved plums, chopped
1cm/½in piece fresh root ginger, grated or cut into matchsticks
¼ onion, thinly sliced
¼ each green and red pepper, deseeded and sliced
2 tbsp light soy sauce
1 tbsp oyster sauce
½ tsp sugar
2 spring onions/scallions, white parts left whole and tops shredded
1 small handful coriander/cilantro leaves, to garnish

1 **RINSE** and dry the fish. Slash the whole fish three times on each side.

2 **PLUNGE** the banana leaf into boiling water to clean it and make it pliable. Cut it into two 30cm/12in squares and stack these on a lightly oiled plate that will fit into a steaming basket or on a trivet, whichever you are using. Place the fish on the squares.

3 **SCATTER** the chopped plums over the fish with the ginger, onion and peppers. Mix together the soy and oyster sauces, sugar and oil, then spoon over the fish. Top with the white parts of the spring onions/scallions. Fold into a loose parcel and secure with cocktail or satay sticks.

4 **LIFT** the plate into a wok or steamer over boiling water and cover closely with a lid. Steam for 8–10 minutes for fillets or 15 minutes for a whole fish, or until the fish is tender. Test with a skewer in the thickest part.

5 **LIFT** out of the steamer and serve on the cooking plate, garnished with the shredded spring onion tops and the coriander/cilantro leaves.

Steamed Stuffed Crabs

Poo-Jar

Crab meat blended with pork, coriander/cilantro, ginger and garlic, packed into crab shells,
then steamed before being served on a bed of lettuce with a piquant sauce. The recipe tells
you how to dress crabs yourself if you need to.

**Serves 4 • Preparation time: 20 minutes
• Cooking time: 10–15 minutes**

4 small cooked crabs (about 200g/7oz each),
    ready-dressed if available
175g/6oz finely minced/ground pork
3 coriander/cilantro stems
1cm/½in piece fresh root ginger, finely
    chopped
2 garlic cloves, crushed
1–2 tbsp fish sauce
freshly ground black pepper
1 egg, separated
lettuce leaves, to serve

FOR THE SAUCE
2–3 red or green chillies, deseeded and sliced
juice of 1 lemon
1 tbsp sugar
6 tbsp fish sauce

1 **REMOVE** the crab claws, place each crab on its back with the head away from you. Use your thumbs to push the body from the main shell. Discard the stomach sac and lungs (sometimes called "dead men's fingers") and any green matter.

2 **SCOOP** out all the edible meat into a bowl and add the meat from the cracked claws. (If the crabs are ready-dressed, all this will have been done for you; simply scoop the meat into a bowl.)

3 **ADD** the pork, coriander/cilantro stalks and some of the leaves with the ginger, garlic, fish sauce and pepper, then mix well.

4 **BEAT** the egg white lightly and use this to bind the pork mixture, then spoon the stuffing neatly into the crab shells. Brush the egg yolk over the stuffing to seal.

5 **PREPARE** the sauce by pounding the chillies with the lemon juice, sugar and fish sauce to taste using a pestle and mortar. Pour into a bowl.

6 **PLACE** the crabs in a steamer basket or on a trivet over boiling water, cover and steam for 10–15 minutes.

7 **SERVE** with some lettuce leaves on a dish and garnish with the remaining coriander leaves. Hand around the sauce to drizzle on top of each crab as it is eaten.

Grilled Whole Fish with Hot and Sour Chilli Sauce

Pla Pow

Whole pomfret or mackerel, smothered in a garlic, coriander/cilantro and oyster sauce, then grilled/broiled to a deep caramel colour and served with chilli sauce. Use whole fish as it looks much more attractive – an important aspect of Thai cuisine.

Serves 4 • Preparation time: 10 minutes, plus 30 minutes marinating time
• Cooking time: 8–10 minutes

2 pomfret or mackerel (350g/12oz each), cleaned
4 coriander/cilantro stems
2 garlic cloves
1 tsp freshly ground black pepper
4 tbsp oyster sauce
1 small handful mint leaves, to garnish
lime wedges, to serve

FOR THE HOT AND SOUR CHILLI SAUCE
5 tbsp fish sauce
juice of 2 limes or lemons
2–3 bird's eye chillies, deseeded, if liked, and finely sliced
2 tbsp palm (jaggery) or light brown sugar

1 **RINSE** and dry the fish and slash the skin three times on each side so that the flavours will permeate the flesh.

2 **POUND** the coriander/cilantro stalks (reserving the leaves for garnish) with the garlic using a pestle and mortar. Add the black pepper and oyster sauce.

3 **SMOTHER** the fish on both sides with this mixture and set aside to marinate for at least 30 minutes.

4 **PREPARE** the hot and sour chilli sauce by placing all the ingredients in a bowl and blending them together.

5 **PREHEAT** the grill/broiler to high and place the fish on a lightly oiled trivet in a grill pan. Turn the grill down to medium and place the fish under it. Cook for about 4–5 minutes on each side, turning once during cooking, making sure the fish doesn't brown too quickly. (Strips of foil placed under the fish may aid in turning it.)

6 **SERVE** on a hot serving dish, garnished with the mint and reserved coriander leaves and the prepared sauce. Provide lime wedges to squeeze over the fish, which will often be filleted at the table when you order this dish in a Thai restaurant.

Beef with Coconut
Pra Raam Long Song

King Rama had a pool in which he loved to swim. This beef in a creamy sauce surrounded
by freshly cooked greens is supposed to represent his bathing paradise!

Serves 4 • Preparation time: 25 minutes
• Cooking time: 1¼–1¾ hours

2 cans coconut milk (800ml/28fl oz/
  scant 3½ cups)
1 tbsp soy sauce
115g/4oz/¾ cup peanuts, half lightly crushed
1kg/2lb 4oz good-quality stewing or braising
  beef/chuck steak, sliced across the grain
  into even-size pieces
6 shallots or 1 onion, sliced
6 garlic cloves, sliced
2.5cm/1in piece fresh root ginger, cut
  into matchsticks
1 lemon grass stem, lower 6cm/2½in sliced
1 tsp chilli powder
1 tbsp dark brown sugar
1–2 tbsp fish sauce
450g/1lb spinach, curly kale or
  mustard greens
1 red chilli, shredded, to garnish

1 **RESERVE** half of one can of coconut milk and place the remainder plus
200ml/7fl oz/generous ¾ cup water in a large saucepan with the soy
sauce and whole peanuts.

2 **ADD** the meat and slowly bring to the boil, then turn the heat down,
cover the pan and simmer gently for 1–1½ hours until the meat is tender.

3 **PLACE** the shallots or onion, garlic, ginger and slices of lemon grass in a
food processor with the chilli powder and blend to a paste.

4 **TEST** the beef with a skewer. About 20 minutes before the cooking time
is up, spoon half the reserved coconut milk into a wok and heat gently
until bubbling. Add the spice paste to this, stirring all the time to bring
out the full flavours.

5 **ADD** this mixture to the beef in the pan and continue to cook for a
further 15 minutes. Add the sugar and fish sauce to taste.

6 **PLUNGE** the spinach leaves, kale or mustard greens into a saucepan of
boiling water, then drain thoroughly and arrange on the serving dish.
Spoon the meat and sauce onto the greens and scatter with the lightly
crushed peanuts. Top with the remaining coconut milk and garnish with
the shredded chilli.

Thai-style Casserole of Duck
Ped Tun

Serves 4 • Preparation time: 20 minutes, plus 1½ hours marinating time • Cooking time: 1¼–1¾ hours

2.25kg/5lb duck, divided into quarters, or 4 duck portions
4 coriander/cilantro stems
8 garlic cloves
1 tsp black peppercorns
1 tbsp brandy or whisky
6–8 Chinese mushrooms
1 tsp each coriander and cumin seeds
3 tbsp sunflower oil
570ml/20fl oz/scant 2½ cups duck or chicken stock (see page 23)
2 tbsp light soy sauce
1 tbsp dark soy sauce
salt
3 tbsp cornflour/cornstarch, blended to a paste with 6 tbsp water

1 **WASH** and dry the duck, then cut into 2 breast and 2 leg portions, if whole. Use the carcass to make stock.

2 **CRUSH** the coriander/cilantro stalks (reserving the leaves for garnish) with the garlic and peppercorns using a pestle and mortar and add the brandy or whisky.

3 **RUB** this mixture into the duck portions and set aside to marinate for 1½ hours. Meanwhile, soak the Chinese mushrooms in 300ml/10½fl oz/ 1¼ cups water for 20–30 minutes, then drain, reserving the soaking liquid. Discard the mushroom stalks and slice the caps.

4 **DRY-FRY** the coriander and cumin seeds in a hot wok for a few minutes, then pound them using a pestle and mortar.

5 **HEAT** the oil in the same wok and add the duck portions. Fry until brown and sealed on all sides then transfer to a casserole/Dutch oven, add the stock and reserved soaking liquid, the mushrooms, coriander and cumin seeds, soy sauces and a little salt to taste.

6 **COVER** and simmer gently for 1–1½ hours until tender.

7 **LEAVE** to cool, then skim off any fat from the sauce. Lift the duck from the stock and discard the skin. Divide each portion in half.

8 **REHEAT** the liquid and add the blended cornflour/cornstarch to thicken the sauce, stirring until it comes to the boil. Add the duck and reheat gently. Garnish with the coriander leaves.

King Prawns, Noodles and Mushrooms in a Clay Pot
Goong Ob Mor-Din

King prawns/jumbo shrimp, marinated in a peppery sauce, layered with noodles and straw mushrooms, then baked and served with a fiery chilli and ginger sauce.

Serves 4 • Preparation time: 20–25 minutes • Cooking time: 25 minutes

100g/3½oz bean thread noodles (2 packs)
16–18 raw king prawns/jumbo shrimp (about 450g/1lb), shelled, heads removed but tails on
2 garlic cloves, crushed
2 coriander/cilantro stems
6 black peppercorns and 6–8 fresh green peppercorns, if available
2 tbsp light or mushroom soy sauce
3 tbsp fish sauce
3 tbsp sunflower oil
6 Chinese/Napa cabbage leaves, 4 left whole and 2 sliced
1 can straw mushrooms (215g/7oz) or 115g/4oz button mushrooms, sliced
1 recipe quantity sweet chilli dipping sauce (see page 27)
2.5cm/1in piece fresh root ginger, unpeeled and cut into fine matchsticks

1 **PREHEAT** the oven to 220°C/425°F/Gas 7.

2 **SOAK** the bean thread noodles in warm water for 10 minutes, then drain and cut into short lengths with scissors.

3 **SLIT** the prawns/shrimp along the back and remove the black vein, then put them into a bowl.

4 **POUND** the garlic with the coriander/cilantro stalks (reserving the leaves for garnish), both peppercorns, if using, soy or mushroom sauce and 2 tbsp of the fish sauce. Pour over the prawns and mix well.

5 **BRUSH** the inside of a clay pot or a 1.25 litre/44fl oz/5 cup casserole with some of the oil, then line with the 4 whole Chinese leaves. (This protects the prawns and keeps the dish moist.)

6 **ARRANGE** the snipped noodles, sliced mushrooms and marinated prawns on top and drizzle with the remaining oil. Top with the sliced Chinese/Napa cabbage leaves, cover with a lid and bake in the preheated oven for 25 minutes.

7 **MIX** the dipping sauce with the remaining fish sauce and the ginger.

8 **SERVE** the dish at once garnished with the reserved coriander leaves. Drizzle the chilli sauce on top of each helping.

Barbecue Spare Ribs

Khrong Moo Yang

The honey in the marinade tenderizes the ribs, making the flesh meltingly tender.
The dark brown, glossy sauce, flecked with sesame seeds, tastes as good as it looks.

Serves 4 • Preparation time: 10–12 minutes, plus 1 hour marinating time • Cooking time: 40–45 minutes

1kg/2lb 4oz meaty pork spare ribs,
 cut into 10cm/4in lengths by the butcher
1 tsp sesame seeds

FOR THE MARINADE
3 coriander/cilantro stems
185ml/6fl oz/¾ cup clear honey or golden/light
 corn syrup, warmed
1 tbsp dark brown sugar
2 tbsp fish sauce
1 tbsp soy sauce
1 tsp five spice powder
1 garlic clove, crushed

1 **ARRANGE** the ribs in a non-corrosive shallow container.

2 **POUND** the coriander/cilantro stalks finely using a pestle and mortar (reserving the leaves for the garnish) and put into a bowl with the remaining marinade ingredients. Mix well, then pour over the ribs and leave to marinate for 1 hour, turning twice.

3 **PREHEAT** the oven to 200°C/400°F/Gas 6.

4 **ARRANGE** the ribs on a trivet in a roasting pan. Sprinkle with the sesame seeds. Cover the bottom of the roasting pan with 2cm/¾in water.

5 **COOK** uncovered in the preheated oven for 40–45 minutes. Use the remaining marinade to baste twice during cooking to keep the ribs moist and enhance the flavour. The honey in the marinade will give the ribs a lacquered look, so turn the ribs if you feel that they are taking on too much colour before the meat is cooked through, and turn down the oven temperature, if liked.

6 **SERVE** the ribs on a plate garnished with the coriander leaves.

Barbecue Chicken

Gai Yang

Chicken breasts or legs are slashed a couple of times through the fleshy part to allow the Thai marinade to permeate the meat before being roasted or barbecued to golden succulence. This is a recipe you will make over and over again.

Serves 4 • Preparation time: 5 minutes, plus 1–2 hours marinating time • Cooking time: 35–40 minutes

4 chicken portions
1 recipe quantity cucumber salad
   (see page 146)

FOR THE MARINADE
4 coriander/cilantro stems
1 tbsp coriander seeds
2 tbsp golden/light corn syrup or
   clear honey
1 tsp black peppercorns, coarsely ground
2–3 garlic cloves, crushed
2 tbsp fish or light soy sauce
2 tsp ground turmeric

1 **SLASH** the chicken pieces and place in a non-corrosive container.

2 **POUND** the coriander/cilantro stalks finely using a pestle and mortar (reserving the leaves for the garnish) and dry-fry the coriander seeds in a frying pan for 2 minutes before crushing.

3 **PLACE** the coriander stalks and seeds in a bowl with the remaining marinade ingredients. Mix well, then pour over the chicken pieces, cover and leave to marinate for 1–2 hours, turning several times.

4 **PREHEAT** the oven to 190°C/375°F/Gas 5.

5 **ROAST** the chicken pieces in the preheated oven for 35–40 minutes in a roasting pan, or barbecue or grill/broil, turning frequently until tender and golden. (Alternatively, you could part-cook the meat in the oven for 25–30 minutes, then transfer to the barbecue for excellent results.)

6 **SERVE** the chicken garnished with the reserved coriander leaves and accompanied by the cucumber salad.

Coconut Milk Ice Cream
Alsa Khrim Ka-Thi

This sumptuous, creamy ice cream could not be easier to make, and contains very few ingredients. The taste of coconut, which is inevitably linked with Thai meals, takes centre stage here, making a suitable end to an oriental meal.

Serves 6 • Preparation time: 12–15 minutes, plus 45 minutes freezing time
• Cooking time: 4–5 minutes

225g/8oz/1 cup caster/superfine sugar
2 cans coconut milk (800ml/28fl oz/scant 3½ cups)
6 tsp toasted desiccated/dried shredded coconut (unsweetened), to decorate

1 **HEAT** the sugar and 125ml/4fl oz/½ cup water in a saucepan and stir over a gentle heat until the sugar dissolves. Continue cooking until the syrup starts to thicken, then remove from the heat and leave to cool for 20 minutes.

2 **ADD** the coconut milk and stir to mix well.

3 **POUR** into an ice cream machine and churn for about 45 minutes, or until you achieve the right consistency. Store in the freezer until the ice cream is needed.

4 **TAKE** it out of the freezer as your guests arrive and let it soften slightly in the refrigerator. (Coconut milk ice cream must be kept cold because it melts rapidly.)

5 **SPOON** into bowls and top with a little freshly toasted coconut.

Fried Bananas
Kluay Tord

Bananas are often underrated as a dessert, but not by the Thais. This dessert is best made while your guests wait at the table, as you can prepare it in no time at all. Try these toffeeish bananas with sweet glutinous rice (see page 174).

Serves 4 • Preparation time: 8 minutes • Cooking time: 5 minutes

4 fresh bananas
55g/2oz/½ stick butter
4 heaped tbsp palm sugar/jaggery or
    brown sugar
juice of 2 limes
4 tbsp coconut milk

1 **PEEL** the bananas and either slice each one diagonally into 4 thick slices or slice lengthways, then halve again for a softer result (as prepared in the weekend lunch with friends menu, page 200).

2 **MELT** the butter in a frying pan or wok and add the banana slices. Fry them on both sides over a medium heat until golden and soft.

3 **SPRINKLE** in the sugar and stir over the heat until it dissolves and thickens to a syrup.

4 **TRANSFER** the bananas and sauce to sundae dishes if cut into slices or on to plates if cut more thinly. Squeeze over the lime juice, drizzle the coconut milk on top and serve.

Glutinous Rice with Mango Slices

Khao Niew Mamoung

This may not be a show-stopper to look at, but that is more than made up for by the glorious balance of coconut-flavoured sticky rice with the golden sun-drenched mangoes cut into arc-shaped slices, topped with shreds of lime rind.

Serves 6 • Preparation time: 20 minutes, plus 1–2 hours resting time

300ml/10½fl oz/1¼ cups coconut milk
55g/2oz/¼ cup caster/superfine sugar
good pinch of salt
1 recipe quantity glutinous rice
   (see page 29), cooled to room temperature
2 ripe mangoes
lime rind, shredded thinly, to decorate

1 **STIR** the coconut milk, sugar and salt together in a bowl until the sugar has dissolved. Pour into a serving bowl, then tip in the cooked glutinous rice. Mix well. Cover and leave on one side for 1–2 hours until the rice has absorbed the coconut milk.

2 **PEEL** the mangoes with a vegetable peeler. Slide a sharp knife as near to the stone as possible while holding the mango on a chopping/cutting board in a horizontal position. Cut on either side of the stone, then slice the mango into long, neat slices. Transfer to a covered container and leave in the refrigerator until required.

3 **SPOON** the rice into individual serving bowls, top with slices of mango and decorate with shreds of lime rind.

Exotic Fruits with Jasmine-flavoured Syrup

Ruam Mit

Tangy oranges, sweet fragrant mango and lychees in a rich syrup, delicately flavoured with jasmine essence, then topped with crushed ice – an unforgettable experience. The jasmine flavour adds an especially exotic touch.

Serves 4 • Preparation time: 20 minutes • Cooking time: 5 minutes

115g/4oz/½ cup sugar
few drops jasmine water, to taste
   (if unavailable, use either rose water
   or orange flower water)
4 oranges, segmented
8 lychees or rambutans, peeled but left whole,
   or can of either (550g/1lb 4oz), drained
1 mango, peeled and sliced either side of the
   stone (see page 178), then cut into cubes
crushed ice
orchid flowers (optional)

1 **PLACE** the sugar and 300ml/10½fl oz/1¼ cups water in a heavy saucepan over a low heat. Stir until the sugar has dissolved, then increase the heat and boil for 5 minutes. Cool to room temperature, then add the flavouring water and chill.

2 **PLACE** the prepared fruits in a serving bowl. Cover and chill.

3 **POUR** the chilled and flavoured syrup over the fruits just before serving. Top with a little crushed ice and decorate with orchid flowers, if you wish.

Pineapple Butterflies
Sub Pa Ros

This is a very attractive yet simple way to serve pineapple. Cover and chill before serving, possibly with the fresh mango (see below). Buy both pineapples and mangoes a few days before you need them to give them time to mature.

Serves 4 • Preparation time: 10–15 minutes

1 ripe pineapple with yellow flesh
banana leaves

1 **WASH** and dry the pineapple, cut off the top and bottom and discard, then cut it in half from top to bottom. Place each half cut-side up.

2 **CUT** a V-shaped groove down the centre of the core of one of the halves.

3 **FORM** the antennae and the top of the wings of the butterfly by making a cut angled toward the centre from both borders of the core. Now make a shallow curving slice from the peel on both sides and remove the flesh from the peel in one piece.

4 **TURN** the pineapple half curved side up. Cut a single groove down the most rounded part of the curve to mark the end of the body and two parallel grooves at equal distances down the sides to separate the wings.

5 **REPEAT** on the other half, then cut the pineapple into 1cm/½in slices.

6 **ARRANGE** the pineapple butterflies on a banana-leaf-lined plate.

VARIATION Fresh Mango *mamuang suk*

Wash 2 ripe mangoes. Place them on a chopping/cutting board and, using a sharp, broad-bladed knife and starting from the stalk end, cut as close to the central stone as possible. Turn the fruit over and repeat. Now you have two perfect halves. Cut in one direction several times close together, then in the same way in the opposite direction to make a criss-cross pattern, taking care not to cut all the way through the skin. With your fingers underneath the fruit, push up and the fruit pieces will rise in a pattern like a hedgehog's prickles.

Oriental Fruit Platter

Polamai Ruam

Here are some of the fruits that might be included in a fruit platter. They will inevitably vary with the seasons, but there will always be enough fabulous fruits to make a spectacular dish. Line the serving plate with a banana leaf cut to fit.

1 banana leaf
2 mangosteens
4 lychees
4 rambutans
1 star fruit

1 PLUNGE the banana leaf into boiling water to make it supple, then cut a piece to fit the serving plate and put it in its place.

2 CUT the shell of the mangosteens all the way around the middle with a sharp knife, being careful not to cut into the flesh of the fruit (the shell is usually about 5mm/¼in thick). Lift off the top of the shell to reveal the creamy white segments nestling in the lower half. Place the opened fruits on the banana leaf.

3 PLACE the lychees on the plate as they are. (To eat, simply crack them open with your fingers and pull them apart to reveal the opalescent fruit around a large brown stone.)

4 CUT the rambutans around the middle, remove the top and display the fruit rather like a boiled egg in a hairy cup. (To eat, hold the bottom part in your fingers and pull out the fruit with your teeth. There is a brown stone in the centre.)

5 CUT the star fruit, or carambola, into horizontal slices to preserve its star shape, and add to the plate.

Pumpkin Filled with Coconut Custard

Sangkaya Phak Thong

The bright orange pumpkin flesh contrasts with the creamy coconut custard filling to create a spectacular dessert. This is a popular sweet throughout Thailand.

Serves 4–6 • Preparation time: 20 minutes, plus overnight chilling time
• Cooking time: 30 minutes

1 small, firm whole pumpkin, about 20cm/8in in diameter (1kg/2lb 4oz in weight); choose a size that will fit in your steamer
4 eggs
150ml/5fl oz/²/₃ cup coconut milk, slightly warmed
2 tbsp palm (jaggery) or white sugar

1 **CUT** the top from the pumpkin carefully and remove the cap to expose the seeded centre. Spoon out the seeds and some of the flesh to ensure the custard mixture will just fill the cavity. Be careful you do not cut through the flesh at the base. If it is tough, pre-steam the pumpkin for 10 minutes upside down. Drain well.

2 **PLACE** the pumpkin on two strips of foil to make it easier to lift in and out of the steamer.

3 **BEAT** the eggs with the slightly warmed coconut milk and sugar until well blended. Strain through a sieve/fine-mesh strainer into a large measuring jug/cup.

4 **POUR** the coconut mixture into the pumpkin, but do not replace the cap. Place the pumpkin in the steamer over boiling water for 20–30 minutes, or until the custard is set and the pumpkin flesh is cooked. Test with a skewer: it should come out clean.

5 **REMOVE** the pan from the heat and allow to cool before lifting the pumpkin out of the pan using the foil straps.

6 **COVER** and chill overnight. Cut into wedges to serve with a selection of fresh fruit slices or a sorbet/sherbet.

Mango Sorbet
Mamuang

Eating a golden mango is like tasting liquid sunshine, and this simple sorbet/sherbet
makes the most of its golden colour and fragrant taste.

**Serves 6 • Preparation time: 15 minutes, plus
1¼ hours cooling time and up to 7 hours
freezing time • Cooking time: 8 minutes**

2 large mangoes (about 450g/1lb each), peeled
85g/3oz/²/₃ cup sugar
5cm/2in piece fresh root ginger, peeled,
   half bruised and the other half cut into
   fine matchsticks
2 limes, rind shredded and juice squeezed
1 large egg white, lightly beaten

1 **PLACE** the mangoes on a chopping/cutting board and slice from
stalk end to tip with the flat of a knife, as close to the stone as possible
on both sides. Place the flesh in a food processor and blend to a
smooth purée.

2 **PLACE** the in a saucepan with 150ml/5fl oz/²/₃ cup water and the bruised
piece of ginger and heat to release the flavour, stirring until the sugar
dissolves. Simmer for 3–4 minutes, then remove from the heat and leave
to cool for 10 minutes. Lift out the ginger and add the lime juice and
matchsticks of ginger to the syrup. Cool for at least 1 hour.

3 **POUR** boiling water over the lime rind in a saucepan and bring to the
boil. Strain and leave to cool, reserving the lime shreds. Blend the mango
purée and syrup together. Continue, following step 4 if you have an ice
cream maker or step 5 if you do not.

4 **POUR** the mixture into an ice cream maker and churn until the mixture
begins to thicken. Add the egg white and churn for 10 minutes more,
then turn into a container and keep in the freezer until required.

5 **POUR** the mixture into a container and place in the freezer for about
2 hours. Remove and use a heavy whisk/beater or large fork to break
down the crystals. Refreeze and repeat after 1 hour and again after 2
hours. Add the egg white, then freeze for another 2 hours before serving.

6 **SERVE** decorated with the lime shreds.

Thai Rubies in Sweetened Coconut Milk

Tup Tim Krob

Red rubies, green emeralds or blue sapphires: the choice is yours for this popular dessert.
Just use the appropriate food colouring for the tiny cubes of water chestnut.

**Serves 4 • Preparation time: 15 minutes,
plus 30 minutes soaking time
• Cooking time: 8 minutes**

175g/6oz/¾ cup sugar
½ tsp red food colouring
1 can water chestnuts (225g/8oz), drained
25g/1oz/¼ cup tapioca flour
1 can coconut milk (400ml/14fl oz/1²/₃ cups)

1 **PLACE** the sugar and 200ml/7fl oz/scant 1 cup of water in a saucepan and stir over a high heat until the sugar dissolves, then reduce the heat and simmer for 3 minutes. Set aside to cool.

2 **ADD** the food colouring to 125ml/4fl oz/½ cup water.

3 **DICE** the water chestnuts by cutting them in three each way to make even-size pieces. Place in the coloured water. Leave for 30 minutes to take on a good colour, then drain thoroughly in a metal sieve/fine-mesh strainer.

4 **SPOON** the tapioca flour into a plastic bag. Add the water chestnuts and toss until the dice are evenly coated. Turn into a sieve/strainer to remove the excess flour.

5 **BRING** a large pan of water to a full rolling boil. Tip in the coloured water chestnuts. Stir lightly to prevent the "rubies" sinking. After 1–2 minutes the "rubies" will come to the surface. Carefully drain in a colander, then turn immediately into a bowl of iced water to cool.

6 **MIX** the coconut milk and the cooled sugar syrup together in a bowl or large measuring jug/cup, then pour into serving bowls when ready to serve. Spoon in the "rubies" at the last minute and serve.

THE MENUS

With so many wonderful dishes to choose from, cooking a Thai meal might seem a bit daunting. Which dishes go with which? How many dishes should be served? To help you plan and cook a Thai meal, I have put together a number of suggestions. Each has a time plan to assist in organizing your time and some hints on what you can do beforehand to prepare ingredients, so that some dishes can be prepared in advance and only need finishing off just before the meal is served. Handy preparation notes offer hints on certain aspects of preparation.

Once you have chosen a menu, plan the shopping and check the preparation notes. Read the recipes through and note the preparations that can be made ahead. Before you start cooking, make sure you have all the equipment you need, such as a wok or steamer, to hand, and that all your ingredients are assembled, particularly if you are going to cook a stir-fry.

Set the table with forks and spoons (never knives, as they are considered weapons). Line dishes with banana leaves and place orchids in a bowl. (Such attention to detail is a hallmark of Thai cuisine.) Then just enjoy the experience of cooking and sharing the food with your guests.

Simple Lunch

Spicy corn cakes with a hint of lime leaves look very pretty on a lettuce-lined serving dish. The Chiang Mai curried noodle soup is a Northern Thai traditional dish. It's a spicy golden curry served with colourful accompaniments. Follow this with fresh fruit.

Corn Cakes
(see page 57)
Chiang Mai Curried Noodle Soup with Chicken Khao
(see page 70)
Oriental Fruit Platter
(see page 181)

The day before, buy the chicken, skin and joint it and store in the refrigerator. Make the corn cake mixture and store in a covered container to form into corn cakes on the following day if time will be short. Halve all the recipe ingredients to prepare this meal for two.

10.45 ASSEMBLE and prepare the ingredients for the soup; cut the chicken breasts into bite-size pieces and refrigerate in covered containers. Prepare the fruit platter.

11.15 ASSEMBLE and prepare all the garnishes for the soup. Fry the noodles. Place in small bowls and cover with cling film/plastic wrap.

11.45 FORM the corn cake mixture into small cakes. Place on a well-floured baking sheet to prevent sticking.

12.00 MAKE the sweet chilli dipping sauce or Thai relish.

12.15 COOK the soup to the end of step 3.

12.40 FRY the corn cakes, drain on paper towels and keep warm in the oven.

13.15 SERVE the corn cakes with the dipping sauce or relish.

13.30 FINISH the soup and serve with the garnishes.

14.00 SERVE the fruit platter.

PREPARATION NOTES

Buy a whole chicken for a dish, rather than chicken portions. This is not only better value but also provides you with food for other meals. Cut each breast portion off the breastbone, and sever both legs where they are joined to the carcass, giving you 4 generous portions. Freeze any pieces you aren't using that day, and use the carcass to make stock.

Lunch Box

Tired of sandwiches in the office? Then take a little time to make this tasty lunch box. The salad, full of tender beef strips and crunchy vegetables, is partnered by steamed fragrant rice and moreish coconut crisps – perfect for nibbling on. Fresh fruit completes the meal.

Coconut Crisps
(see page 61)
Thai Beef Salad
(see page 81)
Steamed Rice
(see page 30)
Fresh Fruit
(see suggestions on page 181)

PREPARATION NOTES
Shake the coconut before you buy it to check that it is full of juice and not cracked. Use a food processor fitted with a sharp slicing blade to get really fine slices. Buy good-quality beef fillet/filet mignon, organic if possible. This cut is known for its tenderness and leanness and is well suited to being pan-fried or grilled/broiled, as in this recipe. Grill/broil the beef to your taste. Leaving it to rest before slicing it helps the meat to stay juicy. Cut it as thinly as you can.

The day before, open the coconut, slice and freeze any coconut slices not required. Keep the crisps for the lunch box in a covered container in the refrigerator to cook the next day. Cook the steamed rice and leave to cool. Cook the beef to your taste, rare or medium, and leave to cool. Prepare all the ingredients for the beef salad and also the dressing. Place in separate covered containers and refrigerate overnight. Note that the recipes used serve four people, so you will need to adjust the quantities to serve just one.

07.20 PREHEAT the oven and cook the coconut crisps.

07.25 MIX all the salad ingredients and pour over the dressing.

07.50 WASH the fresh fruit, if necessary. Remove the coconut crisps from the oven and leave to cool.

08.00 PACK the beef salad, coconut crisps, rice and fruit into suitable covered containers, and remember to pack a fork.

Mid-Week Lunch with Family

Thai fried rice is a popular dish, which looks good served straight from the wok. Meaty spare ribs partner the rice perfectly, and the green mango salad has layers of delicious, spicy textures. Fresh pineapple butterflies round off a show-stopping meal.

Thai Fried Rice
(see page 32)

Barbecue Spare Ribs
(see page 166)

Green Mango Salad
(see page 97)

Pineapple Butterflies
(see page 178)

PREPARATION NOTES

Cook the rice for the Thai fried rice the day before the meal, so that you start with cold pre-cooked rice, which gives the best result. Choose the meatiest ribs you can find (some have scarcely any flesh on them). Buy the pineapple several days ahead to give it time to ripen and so develop its full flavour.

The day before, make up the marinade for the spare ribs. Cook the rice for the Thai fried rice, cool and store in the refrigerator overnight in an airtight container.

10.50 **PLACE** the spare ribs in the marinade, making sure they are well coated, and refrigerate in a covered container.

11.00 **ASSEMBLE** and prepare all the ingredients for the fried rice. Cook the omelettes, roll up and set aside.

11.25 **ASSEMBLE** and prepare all the ingredients for the mango salad, including cutting the mango into shards.

11.45 **CUT** the pineapple into butterflies and cut suitably sized pieces of banana leaf to serve them on. Arrange on a serving dish.

12.15 **PUT** the spare ribs on a trivet in a pan, pour in water and place in the oven. Make the mango salad but toss it together only at the last minute.

12.55 **COOK** the Thai fried rice to the end of step 4.

13.15 **FINISH** the Thai rice and serve with the spare ribs followed by salad.

13.45 **SERVE** the pineapple butterflies.

Mid-Week Lunch with Friends

Tender morsels of chicken and pork satay, served with a crunchy peanut sauce, make the perfect start to a meal that continues with a creamy steamed fish curry, fluffy fragrant rice and crunchy stir-fried vegetables. Golden mango, presented Thai style, makes a refreshing dessert.

Chicken and Pork Satay
(see page 45)

Khun Nan's Steamed Fish Curry
(see page 113)

Steamed Rice
(see page 30)

Mixed Stir-fry Vegetables
(see page 89)

Fresh Mango
(see page 178)

PREPARATION NOTES

Check whether you can buy a banana leaf. Cut out a couple of rounds as described and blanch in boiling water. Practise making the banana cups (see page 26), which are worth the effort.

The day before, cut the discs for the banana leaf cups, allowing two for each cup, and prepare the cups (see page 26). Slice the meats for the satay; cover and refrigerate.

10.40 **MAKE** the peanut sauce and marinade for the satay. Pour the marinade over the meat. Soak some bamboo or wooden skewers.

11.20 **PREPARE** the fish and set in a covered container in the refrigerator. Make the curry mixture, cover and keep cool. Prepare a garnish of shredded lime leaf and red chilli. Set aside in a little coconut milk.

11.40 **STEAM** the rice. When cooked, leave it in the steamer or transfer to a bowl ready for reheating (see page 29), and set aside.

11.45 **PREPARE** the vegetables while the rice is steaming. Thread the chicken and pork pieces onto separate skewers.

12.05 **CUT** the mangoes, cover and chill.

12.25 **FILL** the banana cups at the last minute and secure in a steamer with crumpled foil to keep them steady (see recipe directions); alternatively, use large ramekins. Start to cook as the guests arrive – the cups can be left in the steamer after cooking to keep warm.

13.00 **COOK** the stir-fry vegetables, reheat the rice and serve. Serve the steamed curry garnished with coconut milk, lime leaf and red chilli.

13.15 **COOK** the satay and serve with peanut sauce and cucumber salad.

13.45 **SERVE** the fresh mango.

Weekend Lunch with Family

Ever-popular prawn/shrimp toasts, crisp and crunchy, are firm favourites. They look and taste fabulous. Classic green chicken curry, with its creamy coconut and homemade green curry paste, is memorable served with Thai fragrant rice and spicy crunchy beans.

Prawn Toasts
(see page 38)

Green Chicken Curry
(see page 105)

Steamed Rice
(see page 30)

Spicy Green Beans
(see page 93)

Glutinous Rice with Mango Slices
(see page 174)

PREPARATION NOTES

Buy the mangoes a few days before so they can ripen fully. Leave the cooked glutinous rice to stand in the coconut milk for up to 2 hours so that it has time to absorb all the liquid. Cut the mango away from the stone very carefully, then peel and cut it lengthways into attractive slices.

The day before, soak the glutinous rice overnight or for 12 hours, then steam; prepare the coconut mixture, add the rice to absorb it, then cool and refrigerate in a covered container. Make the Thai relish.

11.20 **PREPARE** the prawn toasts and place on a tray lined with baking parchment. Cover loosely with cling film/plastic wrap and refrigerate.

11.50 **SLICE** the chicken and refrigerate in a container. Prepare all the green curry ingredients; keep the chicken refrigerated.

12.15 **ASSEMBLE** the ingredients for the spicy beans.

12.25 **STEAM** the rice. When cooked, leave in the steamer or transfer to a bowl ready for reheating (see page 29), and set aside.

12.30 **PEEL** and slice the mango while the rice is cooking. Arrange the glutinous rice on plates with the mango and lime on top, cover lightly.

13.00 **COOK** the green chicken curry to the end of step 5.

13.15 **COOK** the prawn toasts and serve with the Thai relish.

13.30 **FINISH** the chicken curry, reheat the rice, cook the beans and serve.

14.00 **SERVE** the glutinous rice with mango slices.

Weekend Lunch with Friends

Seafood in coconut soup zipped up with torn red chilli puts the appetite on alert. The rice salad, a stunning display of separate ingredients on a large dish, is served with crisp barbecued chicken. Melt-in-the-mouth fried bananas, a Thai favourite, complete this lunch in style.

Mixed Seafood and Coconut Soup
(see page 74)

Rice Salad
(see page 31)

Barbecue Chicken
(see page 169)

Fried Bananas
(see page 173)

PREPARATION NOTES

Buy the freshest fish you can find. Choose chunky cod fillets, to produce satisfactory cubes. Score the squid flesh before cutting it into strips to help the flesh curl as it cooks. Choose juicy, plump prawns/shrimp for the best flavour. Store all the seafood in a covered container in the refrigerator.

The day before, make the chilli sauce to drizzle over the salad and store in a screw-top glass jar. Make the marinade for the chicken.

10.30 PREPARE the squid, assemble the fish and refrigerate in a covered container. Prepare the coconut and turmeric for the soup.

11.15 MARINADE the chicken pieces in a glass or stainless steel container. Cover with cling film/plastic wrap, turning the pieces from time to time for an hour.

11.30 ASSEMBLE and prepare all the salad ingredients.

11.50 ARRANGE the salad ingredients around a mound of rice on a large serving dish with the dressing in a separate bowl.

12.00 ASSEMBLE the ingredients for the fried bananas.

12.15 COOK the chicken pieces.

12.30 HEAT the liquid ingredients for the soup with the spices and leaves. Add the coconut and turmeric mixture and the remaining ingredients. Set on one side.

13.00 ADD the fish to the soup once the guests are seated at the table.

13.35 SERVE the rice salad and sauce and the garnished barbecued chicken with the cucumber salad.

14.00 COOK and serve the fried bananas.

Simple Dinner

Nibble on prawn crackers/shrimp chips while waiting for mussels on a bed of herbs. The sweet-sour-salty Thanying salad is rounded off with coconut ice cream. Halve the ingredients to prepare this meal for two.

Prawn Crackers
(see page 53)

Steamed Mussels with Lemon Grass and Basil
(see page 153)

Thanying Salad
(see page 82)

Steamed Rice
(see page 30)

Coconut Milk Ice Cream
(see page 170)

The day before, make the coconut milk ice cream. Cook the chicken for the salad, then cool and refrigerate it in a covered container.

17.00 **SCRUB** the mussels, place in a large container and cover with water until required. Make the chilli sauce for the mussels.

17.30 **ASSEMBLE** all the ingredients for the salad, and blanch the beans. Dry-fry the sesame seeds. Pound the ingredients for the dressing.

18.15 **STEAM** the rice. When cooked, leave in the steamer or transfer to a bowl ready for reheating (see page 29), and set aside.

18.20 **TOAST** or dry-fry the desiccated/dried shredded coconut to decorate the ice cream.

18.30 **FRY** the prawn crackers and drain well on paper towels. Make the sauce or relish.

19.00 **TOSS** the cucumber, dressing ingredients and peanuts together, then fold in the remaining ingredients and cover with cling film/plastic wrap. Put the coconut ice cream in the refrigerator to soften.

19.15 **SERVE** the prawn crackers.

19.25 **COOK** the mussels. Lift onto serving plates, discard the herbs and add the sauce to the juices in the wok. Heat and pour over the mussels. Garnish with basil leaves. Place a separate bowl in the centre of the table for the mussel shells.

19.40 **SERVE** the salad garnished with coriander/cilantro and sesame seeds, with lettuce and rice.

20.00 **SERVE** the coconut milk ice cream.

Romantic Dinner

The prettiest do-it-yourself appetizer, full of colour and texture, is followed by indulgent scallops, fluffy steamed rice and crunchy vegetables. A golden sorbet/sherbet ends the meal.

Lettuce Parcels
(see page 58)

Stir-fry Scallops with Chilli and Basil Leaves
(see page 134)

Steamed Rice
(see page 30)

Baby Corn and Sugar Snaps with Ginger and Garlic
(see page 86)

Mango Sorbet
(see page 185)

PREPARATION NOTES

Choose fresh scallops that are pale beige to creamy pink. (You may need to order them in advance, or at least check when they will be in stock.) Frozen scallops are whiter in colour. Thaw frozen ones overnight in a covered container in the fridge. Cook the scallops only until they turn opaque, which means they are done. Longer cooking will only toughen them, spoiling their delicate taste and texture.

The day before, make the mango sorbet. Put the scallops in a container in the refrigerator to thaw, if frozen. Halve all the recipe ingredients to prepare this meal for two.

18.00 **ASSEMBLE** and prepare the ingredients for the stir-fry scallops. Prepare the ingredients for the lettuce parcels.

18.30 **STEAM** the rice. When cooked, leave in the steamer or transfer to a bowl ready for reheating (see page 29), and set aside.

18.35 **ASSEMBLE** and prepare the ingredients for the baby sweetcorn stir-fry while the rice is cooking.

19.00 **TAKE** the sorbet out of the freezer. Place in the refrigerator to soften.

19.45 **SERVE** the lettuce parcel ingredients, for each person to assemble.

20.00 **REHEAT** the rice while stir-frying the vegetables. Turn into warmed dishes, then stir-fry the scallops and serve.

20.30 **SERVE** the mango sorbet decorated with lime shreds.

Mid-Week Dinner with Family

Delicious, crispy-wrapped prawns/shrimp are followed by a slow-cooked pork curry, crunchy stir-fried vegetables and fragrant rice. The stunning dessert adds a triumphant note.

Prawns in Blankets
(see page 49)

Northern Thai Curry with Pork and Ginger
(see page 102)

Steamed Rice
(see page 30)

Stir-fry Broccoli and Carrots with Bean Curd and Peanuts
(see page 90)

Pumpkin Filled with Coconut Custard
(see page 182)

The day before, prepare the stuffing for the prawns in blankets and thaw the wrappers. Make the curry, so that the flavours develop. Prepare and steam the coconut custard in pumpkin. Cool and place in a deep dish or bowl using foil straps. Cover and refrigerate.

17.50 **MAKE** the prawns in blankets.

18.00 **STEAM** the rice. When cooked, leave in the steamer or transfer to a bowl ready for reheating (see page 29), and set aside.

18.05 **PREPARE** the broccoli for the stir-fry and cut the carrot as directed. Blanch the broccoli; when cold, refrigerate in a covered container.

18.15 **ASSEMBLE** and prepare the sauce ingredients for the vegetables. Chop the pork crackling and ginger into matchstick pieces for the curry garnish.

18.30 **MAKE** the sauce for the prawns in blankets. Turn the curry into a saucepan or casserole/Dutch oven to reheat over a low heat on top of the stove.

18.45 **TAKE** the pumpkin out of the container. Cut into wedges and arrange on a serving dish with some fresh fruit, if liked. Cover with cling film/plastic wrap.

19.15 **COOK** and serve the prawns with the dipping sauce. Reheat the rice.

19.30 **STIR-FRY** the vegetables, add the sauce and bean curd. Serve the curry garnished with pork crackling and ginger, the rice and the stir-fry vegetables topped with peanuts.

20.00 **SERVE** the sliced pumpkin with coconut custard.

Mid-Week Dinner with Friends

The subtle flavours of the soup are complemented by the seafood curry and stir-fry beef.
Finish with oranges, lychees and mango in a flower-perfumed syrup.

Clear Soup with Stuffed Mushrooms
(see page 65)

Prawn and Pineapple Curry
(see page 110)

Beef with Broccoli and Oyster Sauce
(see page 117)

Boiled Egg Noodles and Steamed Rice
(see pages 17 and 30)

Stir-fry Green Vegetables with Yellow Bean Sauce
(see page 137)

Exotic Fruits with Jasmine-flavoured Syrup
(see page 177)

The day before, make the dessert syrup and chill. Make or thaw the chicken stock for the soup. Thaw the prawns/shrimp, if frozen, in a covered container in the fridge. Make the stuffing for the mushrooms.

17.00 SOAK the mushrooms, if using Chinese, and remove the stalks. Stuff the mushrooms of choice and leave in the refrigerator.

17.15 ASSEMBLE and prepare the fruits for the dessert. Chill, covered, in the fridge. Crush the partly thawed ice in a food processor and place in a wide box in one layer in the freezer until just before the meal.

17.45 ASSEMBLE the curry ingredients. Make the soup to the end of step 3. Prepare all ingredients for the beef with broccoli. Blanch the broccoli.

18.15 ASSEMBLE and prepare the green vegetables for the stir-fry and make the yellow bean sauce. Place the mushrooms in a steamer.

18.30 STEAM the rice. When cooked, leave in the steamer or transfer to a bowl ready for reheating (see page 29), and set aside.

18.35 POUR the chilled syrup over the fruits in a bowl for dessert while the rice is cooking and move the crushed ice to the refrigerator ready to spoon on top at the last minute with some orchid flowers.

18.45 COOK the curry to step 3. Steam the mushrooms and simmer the soup. Add the remaining soup ingredients, then serve the soup.

19.30 STIR-FRY the beef with broccoli. Finish the curry, reheat the rice, cook the egg noodles (to accompany the beef dish) and stir-fry the green leaves and yellow bean sauce. Serve these dishes.

20.00 SERVE the exotic fruits with syrup and crushed ice.

Dinner Party

Spicy fish cakes, delicate soup, creamy mixed vegetables, fluffy rice and a deep-flavoured Mussaman curry are complemented by the sweet-sour-salty salad. Thai rubies add the finishing touch.

Thai Fish Cakes
(see page 46)

Clear Soup with Wontons
(see page 66)

Thai Mussaman Curry
(see page 98)

Mixed Vegetable Curry
(see page 114)

Steamed Rice
(see page 30)

Market Salad
(see page 94)

Thai Rubies in Sweetened Coconut Milk
(see page 186)

The day before, make up the chicken stock for the soup or thaw if frozen. Make the filling for the wontons, cover and refrigerate. Make up the Mussaman curry to the end of step 5, cool, cover and refrigerate. Make the Thai fish cakes (three per person) and dipping sauce and refrigerate.

16.15 **THAW** the wrappers and make up the wontons (three per person).

16.40 **TAKE** the Mussaman curry out of the refrigerator. Make the red rubies and put in iced water. Make the sweetened coconut milk, pour into a bowl, cover and chill.

17.25 **STEAM** the rice. When cooked, leave in the steamer or transfer to a bowl ready for reheating (see page 29), and set aside.

17.30 **ASSEMBLE** and prepare all the ingredients for the vegetable curry while the rice is cooking. Cook to the end of step 2.

18.00 **ASSEMBLE** and prepare all the ingredients for the salad. Make up the salad to the end of step 2. Have the tomatoes, papaya or cabbage ready to complete the salad. Soak the tamarind pulp, then strain.

18.30 **REHEAT** the Mussaman curry gently in a flameproof casserole/ Dutch oven on top of the stove. Add the final seasonings when hot.

18.40 **FINISH** the vegetable curry.

19.15 **COOK** the fish cakes and serve with the crunchy dipping sauce.

19.30 **COOK** the wontons, heat the stock, serve the soup and reheat the rice.

19.45 **GARNISH** the Mussaman curry, then serve with the vegetable curry and rice. Toss the final salad ingredients together, garnish and serve.

20.15 **SERVE** the Thai rubies.

Drinks Party

This varied selection of Thai delights comprises a whole host of tastes and textures: soft dumplings, crisp rolls, crunchy crisps and crudités, and more.

Thai Spring Rolls
(see page 42)

Steamed Dumplings
(see page 41)

Prawn Satay
(see page 45)

Money Bags
(see page 54)

Nam Prik Sauce with Crudités
(see page 50)

Coconut Crisps
(see page 61)

Prawn Crackers
(see page 53)

The day before, open the coconut and make the coconut slices; put in a container in the refrigerator. Make the nam prik sauce and money bag filling and refrigerate. This menu will feed eight to ten guests.

15.00 **MAKE** the filling for the Thai spring rolls and thaw the wrappers.

15.50 **MAKE** the filling for the dumplings and thaw the wrappers, including those for the money bags.

16.00 **MAKE** the marinade for the prawns/shrimp, then marinate.

16.30 **DEEP-FRY** the prawn crackers/shrimp chips, drain well on paper towels. Put in a bowl and pour the dipping sauces into small dishes. Have deep oil in a pan or wok to be ready for deep-frying later.

17.00 **PREPARE** the Thai spring rolls and money bags and place on a floured plate. Make the dumplings and place on non-stick baking parchment in steamer baskets ready for cooking.

17.45 **CUT** the vegetables into pieces to serve with the nam prik sauce. Arrange on plates with the sauce in a bowl and garnish with coriander/cilantro. Cover and keep in a cool place.

18.00 **PREHEAT** the oven, spread the coconut slices on a baking sheet and cook until golden. Transfer to bowls. Thread the prawns on the skewers. Set on a piece of foil ready to put in a griddle/grill pan to cook. Turn the peanut sauce into a pan to reheat later. Make the cucumber salad unless serving with toast and chunks of cucumber.

18.50 **PLACE** the wok or deep pan of oil next to the hob/stovetop. Set the dumplings in a steamer. Have the kettle ready to boil.

19.30 **COOK** the snacks and serve with the sauces and relishes.

INDEX